92-Biog
Moz

563

DATE DUE

SEP 32 8	APR 3 0		
MAR 1 8	JAN 9 / JAN 2 3		
APR 1	FEB 6		
SEP 29	MAR 6		
OCT 13	MAR 1		
FEB 10	APR 1 4		
FEB 6	APR 30 '81		
SEP 28	JAN 0 4		
SEP 28	APR 27		
NOV	MAY 1 1		
NOV 28	DEC 23		
OCT 2 4	JAN 1 9		
NOV 24	FEB 2		
MAY 15	8:AM 9/22/92		
OCT 19			
SEP 28	NOV 0 8 1995		
DEC 1 1			
DEC 1 1	GAYLORD	PRINTED IN U.S.A.

At the age of six, Wolfgang Mozart was already known
in Europe and England as a musical genius. This is
the story of the triumph and tragedy in the brief life
of one of the greatest figures in the history of music.

MOZART

Illustrated by W. T. Mars

MOZART

Reba Paeff Mirsky

Follett Publishing Company   CHICAGO

© *1960, by Reba Paeff Mirsky*
Manufactured in the United States of America
Published simultaneously in Canada by
The Ryerson Press, Toronto

23456789

Library of Congress Catalog Card Number: 60-13358

To Bashka
and
Samuel M. Waxman

Salzburg

Y ou can come and see your
baby brother now, Nannerl," Papa Mozart called to his four-
year-old daughter. She was practicing on the clavichord, a
narrow boxlike instrument which looked and was played like a
small piano, but with such a quiet sweet tone that it could hardly
be heard beyond the walls of the room. Often Nannerl played
on the harpsichord, too, when there was no need to be especially
quiet. It had a louder, more metallic tone, since the strings were
plucked by a quill rather than struck, when one pressed the keys.
But today it was important to be quiet.

Nannerl was glad to see her father looking so happy about
the new baby; yet, young as she was, she could detect an anxious

note in his voice when he spoke to her. She ran to take his out-stretched hand, and together they softly entered her mother's room.

"Why, he's hardly bigger than my doll!" exclaimed Nannerl. "What's his name, Mama?"

"Wolfgang. Papa will take him to be christened tomorrow morning."

"And," her father continued, "in the cathedral register it will say that Johannes Chrysostomus Wolfgang Gottlieb Mozart was born on January 27, 1756."

"Pray God that our little one live until tomorrow, Leopold," murmured his wife. "He looks as frail as all the other babies who came before and since our Nannerl. If only we may keep this little son!"

Leopold stroked his wife's hand reassuringly. "Perhaps this time, Anna Maria, our prayers will be answered. Wouldn't it be fine if our son grew up to become a musician like me? One day he too may play in the Archbishop's court orchestra; and he could help me teach singing and the violin to the chapel boys. Who knows, he may make our name famous in Salzburg!"

"Is my name in the church register, too?" asked Nannerl, her eyes fixed on the baby.

"Certainly, my child. It says Maria Anna Walburga Ignatia Mozart, born July 30, 1751."

"Oh, what a lot of names!" laughed Nannerl. "Papa, will you teach my little brother to play the clavichord and harpsichord, too?"

8

"Of course, and the violin as well."

"Then why don't you teach *me* the violin?"

"Because you're a girl, dear. The violin isn't an instrument suitable for young ladies." Her father bent down to kiss her chubby cheek.

"Mama, may I hold my baby brother?" asked Nannerl, holding out her arms.

"Not yet, darling. Wait until he's a little bigger and stronger; then you may hold the baby just as much as you like, Nannerl."

"When my brother is bigger, we will play duets for you and Papa every day," declared Nannerl.

Her mother's face was full of loving pride as she looked at her talented little daughter.

As the months passed Anna Maria and Leopold took delight in seeing their tiny son grow plumper and livelier. Whenever the baby saw Nannerl standing beside his cradle, he squealed with especial pleasure.

"Leopold, just see how our little son loves his sister," Anna Maria said happily.

"Yes, and have you noticed how responsive he is to the least sound? He has an unusually keen ear. I am sure he must be very musical."

Often they heard their little fellow burst into sudden laughter and Anna Maria would say, "Our Wolferl is full of fun and loves to laugh. So far, thanks be to God, he is healthy and thriving nicely. But, my dear husband, you must not hover over him as much as you do. The moment you come into the house you have eyes and ears for no one but our son."

"Yes, Papa, and some days you even forget to give me my music lesson," said Nannerl, reproachfully.

"Have I really been neglecting you, dear Nannerl?" Leopold was apologetic. "That won't do at all. From now on I leave Wolfgang to his good mother and to the will of God. Come, let us make some music, Nannerl."

At the first delicate sounds from the clavichord, soft as they were, the baby grew utterly quiet. He seemed to be listening with his eyes as well as with his ears. His face showed pleasure in the sound of the music.

When the music stopped, Anna Maria saw the baby wriggle impatiently; soon the music began again, and he lay absolutely still. Now Anna Maria could hear Leopold explaining something to Nannerl.

Puzzled by the lack of music, Wolfgang looked up at his mother questioningly. As soon as the music began, he smiled happily. Our little son loves music already, thought Anna Maria. I pray that some day he too will be in the Archbishop's orchestra like his father, but in a higher position. Poor Leopold — always second fiddle!

Anna Maria was proud of her husband; not only was he a respected court musician and composer but one of the best music teachers in Salzburg. Now that he was also the author of a book, "A Method For The Study of the Violin," everyone declared it would make him famous.

The preface to the book said, "Only if a person is a good Christian, and has true moral character, will he be a good musician."

Leopold was a pious man. He came from a family of book-binders in southern Germany. His fees at the University of Salzburg had been paid by the Benedictine monks in whose choir school he was educated as a boy, thinking that he would become a priest; otherwise his family could have ill afforded to send him there.

But Leopold loved music above everything, and when he fell in love with Anna Maria, he had decided to become a musician and stay in Salzburg. First he had obtained a position with a nobleman as musician and valet, then, later, a place in the orchestra of the Archbishop Sigismund, the ruler of Salzburg.

Wolfgang was now sturdy enough to toddle through the four-room apartment the Mozarts occupied on the third floor of a stone house; he found his way easily to all the fascinating musical instruments in their household. The building belonged to their first floor neighbor and friend, Lorenz Hagenauer.

As soon as Wolfgang heard Nannerl practicing, he would stand beside her, watching her little fingers fly over the keyboard of the clavichord or the harpsichord with wonder. Already he was interested in the difference between the sweet tone of the former and the more brilliant tone of the latter.

The beautiful sounds Nannerl made filled him with happiness. It was impossible to resist touching the keys. Were they

11

not the secret of releasing the magical sounds which came out of these two marvellous boxes?

Excited at the prospect he put out two stubby fingers and firmly pressed the black keys up and down, his eyes shining in anticipation of the entrancing music he would hear.

"No, no, Wolferl, I'm practicing now," scolded Nannerl. "Papa won't like it if I don't know my music lesson. Go away."

Wolfgang looked up at her, surprised that anyone should speak harshly to him.

He ran to find his mother.

"What is it, little one?" asked Anna Maria, stroking his golden hair.

Wolfgang buried his head in her apron.

"Ah, I know," she comforted him. "Don't be sad, dear, soon you'll be able to play just like Nannerl. Listen! I think I hear Papa's footsteps on the stairs. Quick, let me dry your tears. There! I wonder if he has brought home a surprise."

At the mention of his father, Wolfgang raised his tear-stained face and brightened up. Hand in hand he hurried to the door with his mother and opened it wide. They could hear Leopold coming up the stone steps to their third floor hallway.

Wolfgang was always delighted when he saw his father wearing the red and gold uniform of a court musician, his powdered wig curled on the sides, the hair in back tied with a black velvet ribbon.

As soon as Leopold reached Anna Maria, he handed her his violin case and music so that he could hold out his arms to

Wolfgang, who rushed into them calling joyously, "Papa! Papa!"

"Well, Anna Maria, has our son been a good boy today?"

Before Anna Maria could answer, Nannerl came skipping out to him.

"Good day, Papa. No, Wolferl hasn't been a good boy at all. He interrupted my practicing."

"So-o-o! Well, forgive him this time, Nannerl. Before long Wolferl will have practicing of his own to do. Then he'll not be bothering you. I'm sure he didn't mean to be naughty. Look, I have something nice in my pocket for you and your brother."

2

Salzburg

Anna Maria was knitting stockings for the children. She sat next to a window facing the small square where the fountain that was the source of water for the households nearby flowed abundantly. From time to time she looked out toward the beautiful mountains beyond their Salzach River. Below, in the cobblestone street, she could see Nannerl playing with her friends. Her ribboned pigtails flew out behind her like the reins of a pony as she chased someone. What a big girl she is getting to be! thought her mother.

As she worked, Anna Maria heard Wolfgang singing to himself in his room. She recognized some of the tunes as parts of pieces which Nannerl practiced, but now and then there were snatches of melodies she had never heard before. What were they, she wondered?

Hearing Nannerl's high-pitched voice outdoors, Wolfgang dropped his toys and ran to the room containing the clavichord. This was his chance, while she was out of the way! Carefully he raised the lid of the magic box.

There, revealed before him, were the wonderful black and tan wooden keys that made such thrilling music when the notes were combined correctly. Now that he was almost three years old, it was easy enough for him to climb up on the straight chair placed before the instrument.

Humming to himself, he tried to find the right note with which to begin one of the pieces running around in his head. His small hands struck notes here and there haphazardly, searching for the right note on which to begin.

But something was wrong. He frowned, trying to play just as he had seen Nannerl do. Somehow what he wanted did not come out. He was vexed. It had all looked so easy when Nannerl played. Why couldn't he do it?

Softly Anna Maria came to stand by the door of the music room. She saw his perplexed little face, his eyes staring angrily at the unco-operative keyboard. He began playing again, but he was obviously displeased with the discordant sounds he was making.

Unaware of his mother's presence, he started, stopped, began playing again, determination in the whole expression of his face and body. Suddenly he pressed down several keys together. They

16

made a lovely sound, and Wolfgang's face brightened; his wide smile showed his square baby teeth.

He had just discovered how to play thirds, and with thirds, he seemed to realize, one could play chords. How beautiful they sounded! Even if he could not yet play Nannerl's pieces, he could make up his own tunes and use the thirds as an accompaniment.

Soon Nannerl returned, her cheeks flaming, her nose moist from the cold air. Hearing sounds from the clavichord, she hurried to the music room, but stopped when she saw her mother place a warning finger to her lips. Nannerl was not to interrupt her brother's musical explorations.

Wolfgang's keen ear, however, had already detected a rustle behind him, and he turned around abruptly. When he caught sight of his sister, he slid quickly off the chair.

Nannerl said, "It's all right, Wolferl, you can stay. I'll take off my coat and hat, and then we can play something together."

When Nannerl came back, she said, "Now, Wolferl, here's a game for you. First you must guess what I am playing, then I'll try to guess what you are playing. Are you ready?"

Wolfgang nodded eagerly.

"Listen carefully," said Nannerl.

Hardly had she played two measures when Wolfgang shouted, "I know!" and sang the remainder of the piece for her.

"Your turn now, Wolferl."

To protect her little son from the disappointment of a possible defeat, Anna Maria said, "Don't forget, Nannerl, that Wolfgang is still too young to play like you."

"But, Mama," explained Wolfgang, "I can sing what's in my head and play the notes to go with it."

For a moment he sat thinking, then began humming something. Soon he found the proper notes in each hand for an accompaniment. At first he played the chords carefully, but as he went along, he became more confident and his touch grew strong.

He sang in his piping voice and when he finished the piece, he turned to Nannerl. "Well?"

She shook her head. "I think you've got something all mixed up. I'm sure I never played that."

"Of course you haven't played it," said Wolfgang. "It's a tune I just made up."

"Oh, that's why. It's really quite pretty," said Nannerl. "But I can't guess something I never heard before. Play a tune I ought to know, the way I did for you."

The musical game continued, and Anna Maria went back to her knitting, glad to see her children amusing themselves so companionably. She was pleased that Nannerl was beginning to have some respect for her little brother's musical ability.

A few weeks later, when Leopold returned from rehearsing the boys' choir in the palace chapel, Wolfgang ran up to him.

"Papa, please come and hear me play some of Nannerl's pieces."

Wolfgang tugged at his father's hand, eager to show him what he could do. Leopold sat near the instrument waiting for him to begin.

18

"My hands are still very small so I can only play Nannerl's easier pieces," apologized Wolfgang. "Now, Papa, see if you can guess what I shall play for you."

When Wolfgang had finished playing, Leopold exclaimed "I know!" and named it.

"Good! Now, Papa, see if you can guess which this one is," and he commenced another piece.

Leopold cocked his head to one side, puzzled.

"Have you guessed yet, Papa?" asked Wolfgang.

"No, I give up. Perhaps Mama knows," he said.

She said, "I don't know what it is, but I think I have heard Wolferl play that before. Where did you hear the piece, dear?"

"In my head, of course," laughed Wolfgang, "and I have many more there. If you want to, Papa, you can write them down for me in Nannerl's music notebook so I won't forget them."

Leopold had compiled a music notebook for Nannerl, to teach her exercises and pieces which he himself had written or copied from composers he admired. They were mostly minuets, graded according to difficulty, the easy ones at the beginning of the notebook.

Seeing how impressed Leopold was by their son's musical ability, Anna Maria said, "You know, dear husband, very soon Wolfgang's hands will be big enough to play some of Nannerl's harder pieces, and then he can have music lessons from you too. He will surely want to know how to read music as well as to play by ear, as he does now."

"I wish you would give me music lessons right away, Papa."

19

"Wait a bit longer, my child," said Leopold.

The cathedral clock struck the hour.

"Gracious! Just hear what time it is," said Anna Maria. "Come, pick up your toys, Wolferl, and get ready for bed."

Reluctantly, Wolferl left the clavichord. Then he smiled and commanded his parents, "Follow me while I sing a march and take my toys to my room. One-two-three-four!"

He gathered up his playthings and stamped to his room, loudly singing a march he had composed on the spur of the moment. Leopold and Anna Maria clapped their hands in time to the tune; Nannerl ran to join the enthusiastic marchers.

Dumping his toys into a box in the corner of his room, Wolfgang climbed up on a chair, bent over, and kissed the tip of his father's nose. It was the usual good night ritual.

Left alone with his mother, Wolfgang undressed and kneeled beside his bed in prayer. She kissed him and went out, leaving the door slightly ajar so he could see a flicker of light from the candles.

She saw Leopold in deep thought sitting beside the table, his hands shielding his eyes.

Anna Maria asked anxiously, "Is anything wrong, Leopold?"

"No, my dear, but I am overcome by the great gift and responsibility God has given us. Wolfgang is an unusual child. We must do everything possible to fulfill his great talent. I hope we shall be equal to the great task before us."

"We shall certainly do the best we can; but I beg you, Leopold, do not set your heart too much on our son's musical

ability; you might suffer deep disappointment. Don't forget, our
Nannerl is just as talented, and why not, when the very air our
children breathe is filled with music? They are present when you
and your friends are making music together, or when you are
teaching your pupils singing and the violin, clavichord, and
harpsichord. Even most of our conversation is about music."

"Yes, true enough; but I am sure our son is not like other
children. There is something very special in him, and we must
make it our life's purpose to bring his talent to full flower."

All at once they heard loud singing coming from Wolfgang's
room, and stopped talking to listen. Anna Maria smiled. "That's
the way he puts himself to sleep, composing tunes and making
up nonsensical words to them or to tunes he has heard."

"What are those funny words he is singing tonight?" asked
Leopold, amused.

"It sounds like O-ragnia fia ga-ta-fa, marina gamina, fi fa fu,
O-ragnia fia ga-ta-fa, marina gamina fi fa!"

They both burst out laughing.

Salzburg

3

One evening after supper, Wolfgang's father said to him, "I wonder if your memory is as good as I think it is. I'll play you a minuet and trio you don't know; I want to see how long it will take for you to learn it without looking at the music."

Like a delighted puppy offered a ball to chase, Wolfgang hastened to the harpsichord and stood beside his father.

"Are you ready?" asked Leopold.

Wolfgang nodded eagerly, and his father began to play. When he had finished, Wolfgang begged, "Just once more, please."

From the corner of his eye, Leopold saw how intently he was listening, his attention never wavering.

"I think I've got it now, Papa."

His father got up, and Wolfgang quickly took his place at the instrument. He began well enough, but soon he stumbled. In distress, he turned to his father for help.

"Don't be discouraged, my boy," said Leopold patiently. "I'll show you where you went off. Listen, I'll play that part over again for you. This time I don't think you'll have any trouble with it."

Wolfgang began again. This time he played the music through perfectly. Leopold was so delighted that he called out, "Anna Maria, did you hear Wolferl?"

His wife came promptly at his call, her linen cap a little crooked over her pretty brown hair.

"My goodness, Leopold, doesn't our son ever tire of so much music? All day long either he's playing the clavichord or the harpsichord or singing or making up music. I should think he'd have had enough for today; besides, it's too late for him to be up."

Wolfgang went to his mother, took her hand, and looked up into her face. "Oh, Mama, I *never* tire of music. It's the most fun of anything!"

She smiled. "Very well then, play the minuet and trio for me once more before you go to bed."

Leopold led his wife to a chair and sat down beside her while Wolfgang played. Proudly he whispered to Anna Maria, "God performs fresh miracles every day through this child."

When Wolfgang finished, he stretched and rubbed his eyes sleepily.

"No mistakes this time either, Papa," he said, proudly.

"Bravo!" complimented his mother, standing up to take him to bed.

Wolfgang came over to his father. Putting his arms around his neck, he looked into his eyes and asked, "Do you love me, Papa?"

"What a question! Rather, do you love me?"

"Oh, I do, I love you second to God, and I promise always to take care of you and keep you carefully in a glass case when you are very old."

His father laughed and said, "I hope you'll remember that when you're a man, Wolferl."

As soon as Wolfgang went to his room, Leopold wrote down on the music he had just played, *"This minuet and trio were learned by Wolfgang in half an hour, at half past nine on January 26, 1761, one day before his fifth birthday."*

From now on, Wolfgang as well as Nannerl had daily lessons with their father. Whatever he told them to do, they did gladly, especially Wolfgang, whose appetite for music seemed insatiable.

Months passed. After a lesson one day, Leopold said, "Anna Maria, I have some interesting plans for our children."

"What do you mean?" she inquired.

"Well, as you see, our Archbishop takes absolutely no interest in our talented children. This is a great disappointment to me, so I have decided to take them to play for the Elector of Munich; he has a great love for music and has a wonderful orchestra in his court. He will quickly recognize how remarkable Wolfgang and Nannerl are. It is high time we showed their musical ability outside of Salzburg."

"You're quite right, dear; but first you must ask leave from the Archbishop, or you might lose your position. Music will surely be Wolfgang's life work, but it will be better for him to begin his career a little later than to spoil his father's. And of course we don't need to worry much about Nannerl's future in music. I hope she will marry early."

"Even so, they must both take their music more seriously and work hard. In Wolfgang's case, music comes all too easily; although he sits at the instruments most of the day, so far he seems to regard them merely as his favorite playthings. Tomorrow I shall begin working with them on the program for Munich."

"What will you have them play?" asked Anna Maria.

"Each of them will play solos on the clavichord and harpsichord, and then they will have a few duets together. Wolfgang can also play some of his own compositions."

While they were talking about the journey, Nannerl came to say good night to her parents. As she kissed her father, he asked, "Nannerl dear, do you know how to make a nice curtsy?"

"A curtsy?" She pouted. "From now on am I supposed to make a curtsy whenever I say good night to you and Mama?"

"Of course not, darling," reassured Anna Maria, embracing her. "Your papa is planning to take you and your brother to Munich to play for the Elector; he is a nobleman, so you must learn to curtsy properly."

"Oh, in that case . . ."

Nannerl made a stiff little curtsy to her father.

Leopold and Anna Maria giggled like children.

"Well, my daughter, I see I shall have to teach you to do it properly; and Wolfgang must learn how to make a courtly bow," said her father.

He stood up. "Look, Nannerl, I'll show you how to make a dainty curtsy."

Gracefully, as if he were wearing a voluminous skirt, he held the skirts of his satin coat; then, putting one leg behind the other, he made a slow deep curtsy to his wife.

"Beautiful!" cried Anna Maria and Nannerl, clapping their hands and laughing.

Pretending to be offended by their amusement, Leopold said, "Very well, Nannerl, then let Mama show you how to do it better."

Anna Maria rose, walked to the end of the wooden-beamed room and slowly approached Leopold, looking at him flirtatiously. She spread out her homespun skirt and inclined her head to one side; then putting one foot behind the other she bent so low that her dress swept the floor in a circular motion.

"Now let me do it," insisted Nannerl.

"Perfect!" applauded her parents. "Now good night, darling, and sleep well."

At the door she turned to curtsy to her parents. "Tonight I shall surely dream of marrying a prince. Good night, Mama and Papa."

When she closed the door of her room, Leopold said, "Anna Maria, you had better get the children's clothes ready. They will need something especially fine to wear at the palace concerts."

"Yes, of course," said Anna Maria excitedly. "I'll buy some pretty silk and taffeta tomorrow and call in the seamstress to help."

Leopold came into the room one day while Anna Maria was sewing. He saw that she looked troubled and asked, "Are you feeling well, dear?"

"Oh, yes, but I confess I am worrying about the expense of the trip to Munich. The clothes and the carriage are going to cost much more than we can afford."

"Stop worrying at once," said Leopold. "Our good neighbor, Lorenz Hagenauer, is going to lend us the money for this worthy purpose, for he is greatly impressed by our gifted children; he knows it will be easy for me to repay him from the sums they are bound to earn from their concerts."

"I have also been wondering how you are going to pack the clavichord which they will need for practicing, and also the clothes boxes," said Anna Maria.

"The clavichord is small and will fit easily under one of the seats of the carriage. One of the clothes boxes can go under the other seat, and the second will be tied on top next to the driver. We'll manage everything and ride comfortably, too," said Leopold.

"Will you need me to go along with you and the children on this trip?" asked Anna Maria. "Someone should stay at home to look after the house and the dog and the canary and the plants.

Besides, you know, I never feel comfortable among aristocrats."

"This time it won't be necessary for you to come with us. We shall only be gone three weeks at the most. After all, Munich is less than a hundred miles from Salzburg."

The succeeding weeks were filled with daily music lessons. Wolfgang and Nannerl worked hard on the program they were to give. They were not at all nervous about playing for the Elector, and they were delighted at the prospect of going on a journey to a place they had never seen.

Anna Maria was very busy with sewing, as well as with her household duties. But her chief concern was to see that her lively children were well-fed, warmly clothed, and healthy. She saw Leopold's pleasure in teaching Wolfgang and Nannerl increase each day. He rejoiced particularly over Wolfgang's noticeable progress in compositions in the music notebook.

One afternoon when Leopold returned from the palace chapel early, he found Wolfgang busily writing something with his father's favorite goose quill pen.

"Look here, Wolferl, what in the world are you doing with my best pen?" he asked severely.

"I'm writing a concerto, Papa. The first part is almost finished."

"A concerto? Let me see it."

"Oh, no, not yet, please. It isn't finished."

"Come, let me see it just as it is. I'm sure it must be something very fine," said Leopold.

Wolfgang, always obedient and loving, gave it to him. At

first, all Leopold could see was a daub of notes written over dried ink blots and smudges.

Wolfgang noticed Leopold's brow wrinkle at the messiness of the music paper, and said, "Really, I couldn't help those blots, Papa. Every time I dipped your pen into the inkwell, a drop fell off the point when it touched the paper. Then I had to rub it off with my hand and write over it. I'm sorry it's not neater."

As Leopold studied Wolfgang's composition he began to smile. "Yes, it's a real concerto, no doubt about it, but isn't it too difficult to play?"

"Certainly it's difficult, but that's why it's a concerto. I'll play it for you, Papa, humming the part the orchestra will play with me. One has to practice and work hard at it until it can be played properly. Sit down over there and listen."

Wolfgang sat down at the harpsichord, very serious. Despite the fact that his hands were small, he managed to convey the meaning of the concerto remarkably well. When he had finished, he turned and said, "Of course, when my hands are bigger I'll be able to play it much better."

As Leopold was congratulating Wolfgang on his first harpsichord concerto, there was a knock on the front door. Wolfgang jumped up to answer it.

He opened the door, and called out enthusiastically, "Oh, good evening, Herr Schactner. How is your butter-fiddle today?"

"Good day, Wolfgang. My butter-fiddle is as soft and sweet as ever; how is your own violin?" said his friend jovially.

Herr Schactner, a court trumpeter and violinist, often came

29

to the Mozart house to play music with Leopold.

"My fiddle is in very good health, thank you, Herr Schactner," said Wolfgang, "and very easy to play. Do you know, I can play it all by myself without anyone teaching me?"

"Welcome, Schactner," said Leopold cordially. "What Wolfgang says is true, about his learning to play the violin by himself. I suppose that from watching and listening to me and my violin pupils, he learned more than I realized."

"Pretty clever of him," said Schactner. "Perhaps Wolfgang will be playing string trios with us before long."

"Certainly! Next time you and Herr Wenzel come to play with Papa, I'll gladly play with you," said Wolfgang.

"Come, come, my boy," reproved Leopold. "You have a great deal to learn before you can play with real violinists."

Leopold and Schactner began tuning their violins in preparation for the duets they were to play, paying no attention to Wolfgang, who watched eagerly. Knowing that music must never be interrupted once it has started, Wolfgang softly pulled up a chair to sit as close as possible to the musicians. Tonight he seemed to be watching as well as listening. When they stopped at the end of a movement, he sighed and said, "Really, Papa, it doesn't look hard at all. I am sure I can do it."

Schactner, always kindly, said, "Perhaps by the time you return from your trip to Munich you'll be ready to play with us."

"I doubt it," said Leopold. Actually, he was thinking it was not at all beyond his little fellow, so eager to try anything that had to do with music!

30

Salzburg

4

Anna Maria was just in the midst of giving water to Herr Canary when she heard the clatter of horses' hooves on the cobblestones in the street, a loud "Whoa!" from the driver, and the sound of a carriage stopping in front of her house.

Perhaps Leopold and the children had returned from Munich at last! The three weeks they had been away had seemed to Anna Maria like three years. She sprang to the window just in time to see Wolfgang hop out of the carriage, Nannerl close behind him.

She threw a shawl over her shoulders and fairly flew down the stone flights of stairs. Herr Hagenauer, on the first floor, had also heard the carriage and was coming out of his door when she reached the landing of his apartment.

The moment Wolfgang and Nannerl caught sight of their mother they rushed into her arms, shouting "Mama! Mama!" and almost smothering her with their embraces and kisses.

"My darlings!" cried Anna Maria, with tears of joy at seeing them.

Leopold embraced her tenderly and said, "It's good to see you and be at home, dear Anna Maria."

"Did you have a good time?" she asked the children. "Did you play well and remember to curtsy properly?"

"Let's go upstairs," said Leopold. "It's too cold down here; we'll tell Mama everything when we have changed our clothes and had something warm to eat. Hurry in, children."

He greeted Hagenauer cordially, saying, "Thank you, good friend, for making it possible for us to go on this trip. It was a great success, and I pay you back at once."

Wolfgang nudged Nannerl. "Go ahead and show Herr Hagenauer how nicely you curtsy." He himself made a gentlemanly bow.

"Just like a little prince and princess," said their landlord, beaming admiringly.

Wolfgang and Nannerl entered their apartment and ran straight to the bird cage. Their dog bounded toward them, his tail wagging.

"Mama, thank you very much for taking such good care of Herr Canary — and was Bimperl a good doggie while we were away?" asked Wolfgang.

"He was, indeed," assured Anna Maria, "but he certainly

missed you and Nannerl. All at once he lost his appetite and stopped playing. He was so quiet I was really afraid he was going to be ill."

Anna Maria prepared a hearty supper and, after saying their prayers, the family sat down to eat. The smell of the hot, delicious food sharpened Wolfgang's appetite tremendously. He could hardly wait to be served. With the first mouthful he declared, "The Elector in Munich should have you as a cook, Mama; then he wouldn't be so skinny."

"Hush, Wolfgang!" reproved his father. "That's not a polite thing to say about His Transparency."

Nannerl burst into giggles and said, "Transparency is a good name for him, Mama." She clapped a hand over her mouth to save the dumpling she was eating.

Leopold looked at her sternly and turned to Anna Maria. "Never mind their manners tonight, my dear. Our children are excited at being home again."

When they had quieted down, Leopold said, "I wish you could have heard Wolfgang and Nannerl play for the Elector, Anna Maria. They delighted everyone at court."

"I was sure you would not be disappointed in them, Leopold. But how lonely it was here without all of you!"

"What do you think, Mama, everyone was surprised to learn that Nannerl is only eleven years old, and they thought I was much older than six," said Wolfgang proudly.

Unable to resist teasing her brother, Nannerl added, "And they thought Wolfgang was *very* good, for such a *little* boy."

Wolfgang flushed and stopped eating.

"Don't be unkind, Nannerl," rebuked her father. "You have both done well, but you can do ever so much better if you work hard. Wolferl, finish your supper."

To distract Wolfgang, Leopold said, "I think tomorrow is the day when Herr Schactner comes with his butter-fiddle to play trios with me. Perhaps he'll let you try his instrument. I know how much you like its soft full tone."

Wolfgang's cheerfulness was restored at once. He attacked the juicy schnitzel covered with vegetables.

Until bedtime the children filled Anna Maria's ears with enthusiastic descriptions of Munich and the Elector's magnificent court.

"You should have seen the clothes the nobles wore, Mama!" declared Nannerl.

"And how fancily the musicians were dressed!" added Wolfgang. "Papa says that the musicians in His Transparency's orchestra are better than those in the Archbishop's orchestra here. And just think, the Elector himself is a wonderful cellist."

"He was generous in his praise and in his gifts," Leopold told Anna Maria.

"I am glad to hear it," said Anna Maria, "but the best thing is that you all remained in good health. I worried that the long journey and the excitement of playing for the Elector in Munich might be too much for our children."

When Wolfgang and Nannerl went to bed, Leopold said to Anna Maria, "I guarded our treasures well, you may be sure.

I saw to it that if they were up late at night playing concerts, they spent the morning sleeping or resting. I did not insist they practice on the clavichord until they were well fed and well rested.

"They looked charming, and played so delightfully that everyone fell in love with them. I tried to keep people from paying more attention to Wolfgang than to Nannerl."

"I do hope so much praise and attention won't be bad for him. How did he behave about it all?" asked Anna Maria.

"It's a most remarkable thing, Anna Maria, but he seems utterly unaffected by it. He is a modest, sweet, unspoiled child. As a matter of fact, he was far more pleased when people praised Nannerl's playing. He has a good and generous heart, that little fellow of ours."

"I am relieved to hear this. Tell me, Leopold, don't you think that Nannerl is actually a better performer on the clavichord and harpsichord than Wolfgang is?"

"Yes, at present she is, but he is far more creative; he improvises and composes easily. I expect that when he is Nannerl's age he will play not only as well as she does, but even better, and be a good violinist, too. He tells me he wishes to learn to play the organ. He is fascinated by all musical instruments; but above all, he loves to compose music, and that pleases me very much."

"It was a good idea to take the children to Munich, Leopold. It is good for people elsewhere to hear and see talent that goes unappreciated in Salzburg. How can our Archbishop be so blind to something so remarkable at his very doorstep?"

"I'm afraid there will be few suitable opportunities here for our son. In all the years I have been in the service of the Archbishop, he has done little to advance my position or increase my meager salary."

"The Archbishop is none too pleased that you refuse to be his servant and lackey as the other musicians are. I am proud that you refuse to be servile, Leopold, for you are beyond all of them in education and musicianship." Anna Maria sighed. "I see all too well that we must be prepared for Wolfgang to have a position in another court away from here."

"Perhaps in the autumn I shall take the children to Vienna," said Leopold. "The people there are considered very musical."

"Do as you think best, dear husband. Everyone says Vienna is one of the most musical cities in the world."

"The nobles in Vienna would undoubtedly reward our children handsomely if they thought well of their concerts," said Leopold. His eyes sparkled at the very thought of the triumphs awaiting them.

5

Salzburg

The next evening their good friend, Herr Schactner, arrived to welcome the return of Leopold and the children. As he entered, Wolfgang was absorbed in playing on his small violin, his face filled with the pleasure of the music he was making.

When Wolfgang saw his friend he stopped playing and ran to him, full of affection.

"Good evening, Herr Schactner. Did you bring your butter-fiddle?"

"Yes, of course. Would you like to try it?"

"Thank you, I would, but if it is tuned the way it was when you were here last time, it is half a quarter of a tone lower than mine," said Wolfgang.

"Impossible!" exclaimed Herr Schactner, confounded.

"Oh, yes, it is!" insisted Wolfgang.

"Let's see if he is right, Schactner," said Leopold. "He does have an unusually good ear and memory."

Herr Schactner took out his violin and plucked the A string. Then Wolfgang sounded his A.

"By Jove, he is right," said Leopold, proud of Wolfgang's unerring sense of pitch.

There was another knock on the door. Nannerl ran to answer.

"It's Herr Wenzel, Papa," she announced happily. Herr Wenzel was another court musician, and a cherished family friend.

The cordial greetings over, the men turned to their instruments and sat down before their candlelit music stands.

"By the way, Wenzel, what's that music you have brought with you?" asked Leopold.

"Oh, just some trios I composed while you were away. I should be very grateful if you would tell me what you think of them," said Wenzel respectfully.

Leopold stopped tuning to study the compositions. "You have some very interesting ideas here, Wenzel," he said approvingly. "Let's try your trios first and see if they sound as well played as they do when I read them. I'll play the cello part on my viola, you take the first violin part, and Schactner can play the second violin part."

"What about me, Papa?" asked Wolfgang. "Can't I play the second violin part with Herr Schactner?"

38

"No, Wolferl," said Leopold. "As yet you know very little about the violin. It's impossible for you to play such difficult music. Wait until you know more."

Wolfgang's face fell, and he frowned unhappily. When the musicians tucked their instruments under their chins, Wolfgang tried his father once more.

"Please, Papa. One doesn't need to have learned a lot to be able to play the second violin."

Schactner, the second violin player, tried to hide his amusement at the unintended insult.

Leopold was now impatient with Wolfgang. "Wolfgang, stop being a nuisance. If you want to listen to the music, go and sit down quietly over there."

Wolfgang slowly walked away, a dejected little figure, clutching his smallest-size violin and bow.

"Oh, come, Leopold, why not let Wolfgang play with me?" interceded Schactner. "He can try, can't he?"

Leopold relented. "All right, Wolferl, Herr Schactner says you may play with him; but do it very softly so you're not heard, or I'll send you away immediately."

Wolfgang lost no time in pulling up a chair to sit beside his friend. Tucking his small violin under his chin, he commenced playing with the others at a signal from the first violinist, Herr Wenzel.

Before long Schactner realized that Wolfgang was playing the second violin part more than passably well. Unobtrusively, he stopped bowing and let Wolfgang play the part by himself.

Leopold and Wenzel were not at first aware that he had dropped out. When they finished playing the trios and knew what had happened, they could not conceal their amazement. Schactner and Wenzel applauded Wolfgang enthusiastically, but he looked up at his father and asked uneasily, "Did I do it well enough, Papa?"

"Far better than I expected, my son," said Leopold, trying not to look too proud.

"Well, Mozart," chuckled Schactner, "from now on, I don't think you will need me for second violin parts."

"Of course we will, Herr Schactner," said Wolfgang. "Next time I shall play the *first* violin part with Herr Wenzel, if Papa will let me."

Anna Maria appeared at the door of the music room and beckoned to Wolfgang.

"Come, dear, I need you to try on the new suit I am making for your next concerts."

Wolfgang followed her, holding his violin under his arm and swinging his bow triumphantly. How exciting it had been to play trios!

"You know, Mama, making music is the best fun in the world," he told her. His face was aglow with the joy of his first experience in playing chamber music.

"Anna Maria, do you realize what the date is today?" asked Leopold at breakfast one morning. "It's already the tenth of September. You'd better begin packing the clothes boxes for our trip to Vienna, if we are to leave on the eighteenth."

"Very well, dear, I'll begin getting things ready today. By the way, Nannerl is waiting for you at the harpsichord."

Wolfgang, in his room, was rapturously scribbling the arithmetic tables he was learning on the walls, the floor and on his chairs with white chalk. From the moment his father had begun to teach him arithmetic, he had fallen in love with numbers. When he was not playing the clavichord, the harpsichord or the violin, he was absorbed in the discovery of how beautiful numbers could be. His joy expressed itself by writing them all over his room. What prettier decorations could one possibly have! He invented a club called "The League of Numbers" of which he told Nannerl he was a distinguished member.

After a while Anna Maria called, "Wolferl, Papa wants you to come for your lesson right away."

Wolfgang came out of his room, his hands, face and suit covered with chalk dust.

"Goodness, Wolfgang, have you been making a mess with your numbers again?" asked his mother. "You'd better hurry and get washed before you go to your father."

Wolfgang went to the crockery basin, poured water from a pitcher, and washed himself in a perfunctory manner. Hardly drying himself, he hurried to his father in the music room.

"You're dripping wet, Wolfgang," said his father. "Have you been out in the rain, or did Mama make you wash the arithmetic tables off yourself again?"

Each day, after performing his musical duties at the palace and teaching at home, Leopold spent as much time as possible

42

working with his children. Wolfgang and Nannerl loved their music and were eager to please their adoring but firm father. Wolfgang, particularly, never found making music or practicing tiresome or too long.

At last it was September 18, 1762, the day set for their departure to the great city of Vienna. Anna Maria had carefully packed their court clothes. The carriage was larger than the others, for Mama was going too.

Amid shouted farewells and good wishes from their Salzburg friends, the Mozart family set forth. For a while they sat silently, Leopold holding on his lap Wolfgang's small violin and his own larger one, to keep them safe from the jouncing.

Wolfgang and Nannerl were far more excited about this journey than the one to Munich, when they had gone without their mother.

"This will be a much longer trip, won't it, Papa, and now that Mama is with us, it will be ever so much nicer," said Wolfgang happily.

"If it were not for Herr Hagenauer's kind and generous help again, we would not be journeying in such a luxurious carriage," Anna Maria told Wolfgang and Nannerl, so they would not forget to be grateful.

"Lorenz is a wonderful friend. When I protested that we did not need such an expensive carriage, he said, 'Your family must make a good impression upon your arrival in Vienna, and a fine carriage will be noticed.'"

"If only the Archbishop had as much faith in the ability of

our children as our good friend, Hagenauer, we would not have to be taking long journeys to play elsewhere," said Leopold.

Salzburg was soon behind them. The heavily-laden carriage clattered over the rough, stony roads, sending up swirls of dried leaves and clouds of dust through the windows.

The autumn weather was beautiful. There were poppies in the meadows, rabbits darting across fields, birds flying from tree to tree. Wolfgang and Nannerl peered through the windows trying to see everything.

Soon Wolfgang said, "Papa, do you think the Empress will like us?"

"Why not? If you're good musicians she will be very pleased, I am sure. She herself is said to be an excellent singer, and she has summoned the best teachers, musicians, and composers to her court. The famous composer Gluck is her children's music teacher."

"I hope I won't be too nervous to play well," said Nannerl.

"Don't worry about it, Nannerl, dear," said her father. "Although they say the Viennese are great connoisseurs of music, I am not at all uneasy about you and Wolferl. If you play for them as well as you play for me and Mama, I shall be satisfied."

The journey to Vienna was far longer than Wolfgang and Nannerl expected. The roads were rough and bumpy, full of deep ruts. Sometimes the carriage swayed and bobbed like a small boat on a stormy sea. Each night the Mozart family slept in a different inn along the way.

The beds were rarely comfortable, the food not always very

good; but Wolfgang and Nannerl hardly noticed the discomforts. Everything they saw interested them; people, houses, animals, different foods, strange manners, curious towns and villages.

Usually there was time to practice on the clavichord in their rooms before supper. The tone of the instrument was so dainty it did not disturb the guests in adjoining rooms.

Wherever Leopold knew of a bishop or noble who might be interested in hearing the children play, he would tell the driver to halt. The Bishop of Passau kept them as his guests for five days so as to enjoy the Mozart children's playing.

When their carriage stopped at the edge of a wide river, Wolfgang asked, "What's the matter, Papa? Why have we stopped here? Shall we have to swim across the river?"

Leopold laughed. "No, we have to wait for the ferry to take our carriage across to the other side."

Wolfgang and Nannerl were delighted with the idea of riding in a carriage on the Danube River. As soon as they reached the other side, customs officials approached them, expecting to collect a huge tax from passengers who could afford such a handsome vehicle.

"What's in those boxes under the carriage seats, and on top, next to the driver?" they asked Leopold suspiciously.

The Mozart family got out of the carriage to let the customs men inspect the baggage. Anna Maria thought unhappily of the labor of unpacking and repacking.

Leopold told them, "We have a clavichord under that seat, over here are the children's clothes, and on top are my wife's and mine. In this wooden case I am holding are two violins, and this package contains music. That is all."

Wolfgang came forward sociably and said to the customs inspectors, "We are going to give some concerts. Would you like to hear me play? I can give you a concert on my violin right away, if you wish."

"With pleasure," said the amused officials, no longer interested in inspecting the baggage.

When Wolfgang finished playing, the customs men applauded heartily.

"How old is your son?" they asked Leopold.

"Six," he replied.

"Well, good luck, sir. Never mind about opening the cases. A pleasant journey to you all."

It had taken three weeks to reach Vienna, but the children's spirits remained high despite dust, fatigue, sitting all day in one spot, and sleeping and eating in inns that were often crowded and dirty. Since Mama and Papa were with them, and they had their musical instruments, their music, fine clothes, and high hopes, what more could they wish for?

"If you had one wish now, Nannerl, what would you desire?" asked Wolfgang suddenly.

"Herr Canary. And what would you wish for, Wolferl?"

"Bimperl, our dog, of course," he said.

Vienna

6

The first glimpse of the famous city of Vienna was very different from what Wolfgang and Nannerl had imagined. They were astounded by its size and beauty.

"How many wonderful buildings and palaces and parks and statues there are here!" Wolferl exclaimed.

"And just look at the cathedral and churches decorated with marble angels, cherubs, and saints!" marvelled Anna Maria, as excited as her children.

Leopold found inexpensive lodgings for the family at an inn and immediately set to work to let the proper people know that the remarkable Mozart children had arrived in Vienna and would give concerts. Fortunately their fame had already preceded them; before long there came a royal invitation.

With a sigh of relief, Leopold told his family, "We're very lucky! The Empress has invited us to come to her summer palace in Schönbrunn tomorrow. She says she very much wishes to hear Wolfgang and Nannerl play."

"Hooray!" shouted Wolfgang. "The Empress must have some marvellous instruments to play on. Don't you think so, Papa?"

"No doubt about it, Wolfgang."

Nannerl was already unpacking her prettiest concert dress, the one in yellow satin edged with lace and embroidered with pink rosebuds. She held the dress against herself, looking into the mirror admiringly.

"Will you know the way to the summer palace, Papa?" said Wolfgang.

"The Empress is sending her coach for us. In the morning we must have our hair dressed. Now get a good rest, children, and later on we'll go over the program you will give at the palace."

Early the next afternoon, a magnificent gilded coach, a truly royal carriage, pulled up before the inn in which the Mozarts lodged. A footman in a deep red satin uniform sat beside the driver; another servant, similarly dressed, arms folded neatly, perched stiffly on a single seat attached to the back of the carriage. "I thought he was a statue at first," whispered Wolfgang to Nannerl.

The four Mozarts were dressed in their best clothes, Leopold in a white wig, the rest of the family with their hair fashionably curled and powdered white. Anna Maria, Wolfgang, and Nannerl were helped up the steps of the royal coach by the footmen. Carefully the Mozarts sat down on the crimson velvet cushions embroidered with the royal crest in gold thread; they were speechless at the sumptuousness of their conveyance.

Wolfgang and Nannerl exchanged impressed glances, and Wolfgang whispered to Nannerl, "It's just like something in a fairy tale."

And she whispered back, "I shall *always* remember October 13, 1762!"

Their parents, sitting opposite, could not keep their eyes from returning again and again to their two beautiful, wonderful children.

Wolfgang was dressed like a small court gentleman, with a miniature sword by his side which he touched proudly from time to time. He tried hard to sit still, not to talk; but there were so many questions that arose in his mind that he finally had to lean over and ask his father, "Do you think the palace at Schönbrunn will be as fine as the Elector's in Munich?"

Leopold nodded. "I am told it is far more beautiful."

"Is the Empress very old?" asked Nannerl softly so the footmen would not hear.

It interested Anna Maria to see the children full of such questions, but not at all worried about performing before their Empress.

It was only four miles from Vienna to Schönbrunn; within

an hour, the royal coach halted before tall ornate gates decorated with the imperial crown and arms.

With ceremony, the gates were opened for the invited guests; the carriage drove through a winding road among the most elaborate and carefully tended grounds the Mozart family had ever seen. There were fountains of all kinds shooting jets of water high into the air.

All at once they heard tunes coming from various parts of the garden.

"What's that?" asked Wolfgang, excited.

"Ah, it's exactly four o'clock," said Leopold, glancing at his watch. "The music boxes in the fountains must play on the hour."

The stately trees, the profusion of delightful flowers, the graceful swans floating on the pond nearby, filled the family with pleasure. Wolfgang was overcome by the beauty of it all, and he said to his father, "Oh, I would love to explore this wonderful garden."

The coach stopped before the sweeping outdoor staircase of the pale yellow summer palace, and the footman helped the Mozarts out of the carriage. Keeping close to her husband's side, Anna Maria whispered to him, "The palace looks more like the country house of a nobleman than a queen's palace. It's not half as grand as I expected."

But inside! Enormous rooms led endlessly from one to the other. The walls were covered with paintings, tapestries, full length mirrors reflecting scenes from the garden. Crystal chandeliers dangled from ceilings covered with pictures painted by skillful artists. So busy was Wolfgang looking at the pictures on the ceilings that he forgot to walk in the direction he was supposed to; Nannerl caught his arm in time to keep him from straying into a corner.

There was exquisite furniture made of rare woods, some of it adorned with semi-precious stones. The highly polished floors of inlaid woods were in designs, like the finest cabinet work.

Wolfgang whispered, "Nannerl, wouldn't these floors be great to slide on?"

"Yes, almost as good as skating on ice," answered Nannerl.

Wolfgang wished he could peep into some of the little malachite and agate boxes standing on tables. But they could not stop to look or touch anything. They marched behind the guard leading them to the Empress.

Doors were opened from one room to the next by uniformed lackeys with expressionless faces.

"Where in the world is the Empress hiding, Nannerl?" asked Wolfgang softly.

At last they arrived at the royal suite where they were to be received. Before Wolfgang caught sight of the Empress herself, he was struck by how homelike her rooms were; then he saw the Empress, sitting in a red damask chair.

So warmly did Maria Theresa receive the Mozart family that they forgot how nervous they were. Leopold bowed, Anna Maria and Nannerl curtsied, and Wolfgang went up to kiss the Empress's hand, just as he had been taught to do by his father.

As he did so, she bent over and put her arms about him

like an affectionate mother. Suddenly, to his parents and Nannerl's shocked surprise, they saw Wolfgang climb up into her lap and kiss her cheek.

"Wolfgang!" exclaimed his father, horrified. He hurried to take him down from the Empress's lap.

"Oh, let him be," laughed the Empress graciously, without letting go of Wolfgang. "He's a dear child. I'll send for my husband and three of my younger children, as well as members of the court. I want them all to have the pleasure of hearing your son and daughter play."

"Would Your Highness like to hear me and Nannerl play some four-hand pieces on your beautiful harpsichord over there?" asked Wolfgang, speaking to her as if she were an old friend.

"Yes, Wolfgang, it would be a great joy to hear you. As soon as the others come, you and your sister must give us a concert. My children study music too, and we love it as much as you do."

"That's wonderful, Your Highness; then we shall all be the best of friends!" said Wolfgang enthusiastically.

When the Empress's family arrived, the Mozarts bowed and curtsied again. Wolfgang and Nannerl were asked to play on the Empress's harpsichord. First they played solos, then duets. Then Wolfgang played his violin, accompanied on the harpsichord by Nannerl. They looked very charming together, both so natural, yet already little artists in their approach to music making.

Their obvious pleasure in making music, their ability and

modesty, delighted everyone. Never had the court heard such remarkable talent at so young an age, and in such unspoiled children.

Although Wolfgang, as the younger and smaller, was greatly admired, Nannerl impressed the audience just as much. This made Anna Maria happy, for she always worried about the possibility of rivalry between her children. Above all, she wanted them to love each other and be good friends.

The first concert before the Empress had been a splendid success; Leopold was certain they would be invited to come and play again.

The next morning a huge package came to the inn. "It is for the Mozart family," said the innkeeper respectfully. Wolfgang and Nannerl kept asking, "What's in it, Papa? Who sent it?"

Hardly able to wait for him to open it, they jumped up and down in excitement and curiosity. To their surprise and delight, they found that it was a present from the Empress. They held their breath as they beheld a magnificent court dress of white taffeta, embroidered and hand-trimmed, for Nannerl; a lilac suit bordered with wide gold braid, and even a small jewelled sword, for Wolfgang. Within the package was a note from the Empress. It said, "These garments for Wolfgang and Nannerl were outgrown by my children, Marie Antoinette and the Archduke Maximilian. I hope they will be a useful and happy souvenir of the wonderful concert and the pleasure your children gave us."

In addition there were a hundred gold ducats for Leopold

and Anna Maria. It was a large sum of money, and Leopold and his wife looked at each other thankfully. Now they would be able to repay part of the money they had borrowed from Lorenz Hagenauer for the journey to Vienna. The Empress's gift would also make up for the lack of Leopold's salary from the Archbishop in Salzburg while on leave of absence.

Although Wolfgang and Nannerl were not particularly interested in the gold ducats, they were happy enough to see how relieved their parents were. They immediately began trying on the clothes that had belonged to the prince and princess.

Again Wolfgang and Nannerl were sent for to play for the Empress. This time they wore the beautiful clothes she had sent them. When Wolfgang finished playing his solos, he ran to his father, his face rosy with excitement; suddenly there was a thud as he slipped and fell on the highly polished floor.

Marie Antoinette, who was slightly older than Wolfgang, leaped out of her chair and ran to help him up. She straightened his jacket and smoothed down his hair, looking at him anxiously. Wolfgang was out of breath, but managed to smile, saying, "Thank you, Princess. When I grow up I will marry you, because you are so kind."

Marie Antoinette, who one day would become queen of France, blushed, and led him to his worried father.

"Are you hurt, my son?" he asked solicitously.

"Not a bit, Papa," Wolfgang reassured him.

The Emperor called Wolfgang to him and said, "If you are all right, young man, I wonder if you could play the harpsichord just as well if the keys were covered with a cloth."

Wolfgang answered, "I think so, Your Majesty."

Considering it only a game rather than an obstacle, Wolfgang played as easily on the cloth-covered keys as if he could see the keyboard. The Emperor nodded his head approvingly and said, "Well, I see you are a regular magician. Now, my boy, how about improvising on a musical phrase I shall give you?" He was testing Wolfgang's ability with various musical tricks.

On the few notes the Emperor gave him, Wolfgang was able to compose a lovely piece at the harpsichord on the spur of the moment; his imagination was never at a loss to create something. Whatever he was asked to do, Wolfgang was able to do easily, composing variations to suggested tunes, reading music at sight, adding a part to a song he had never seen before. The court marvelled at him more than ever.

When the performance was over, the Empress said to Leopold, "Thank you for the great pleasure your children have given us. Perhaps they would enjoy going into the garden with my children now."

Wolfgang and Nannerl were delighted to hear this, and flew outdoors with the princesses and the young archduke to walk and play among the trees, statues, and shrubs. At last Wolfgang had his wish, to explore the vast and beautiful grounds.

While they were riding back to the inn in the royal coach, Wolfgang asked his father, "Did we play well enough today, Papa?"

"Yes, I was very well pleased with you and Nannerl; but

55

naturally, you can always do better if you will work harder."

"Did we look nice, Mama?" asked Nannerl, touching her beautiful court dress.

"Every bit as lovely as the princesses," said Anna Maria proudly. "But the minute we get back to the inn, you must put on your everyday clothes."

"Otherwise, you might turn into a pumpkin!" teased Wolfgang.

The fame of the Mozart children spread through Vienna. More and more invitations poured in from noble families, many of whom had their own private orchestras. Family music was so common, so greatly appreciated, that servants were often hired on the basis of whether they played a musical instrument well and could contribute to family enjoyment.

The Viennese aristocracy realized that good company was brought together by the pleasant pastime of music; wealthy families were ever on the alert for the latest compositions by famous composers, or for the arrival of remarkable musicians. There was rivalry to obtain the best performers for their orchestras or for special celebrations.

All too often, the rewards for the performance Wolfgang and Nannerl gave were high praise or gifts of things rather than money. Leopold told his wife, "It would be nice if our children were presented with ducats instead of snuff boxes, watches, and laces. Attractive and valuable though they may be, bills cannot be paid with such things."

"Yes, we have enough of them," sighed Anna Maria.

56

Still, there were ducats in sufficient amount to pay their daily modest expenses, and everything was going well enough. Now and then, however, Anna Maria worried about the late hours her darlings had to keep. They played at the pleasure and convenience of the aristocrats, who often wanted them in the evening and kept them up till two or four in the morning, without consideration of Wolfgang and Nannerl's tender age. One day their mother asked her husband apprehensively, "Have you noticed how tired the children are beginning to look? It worries me."

Not long after this observation, Wolfgang awoke one morning complaining, "Mama, I have a terribly sore throat."

He lay back on his pillow, not trying to get up.

He had often had colds, but they had never interfered with his desire to get up early, to make music and be with people. But today he lay in bed, his eyes red and drooping.

"Look at him, Leopold. Something must be wrong with the child," said Anna Maria.

"I hope not. Perhaps he's only overtired and will soon feel better when he has had enough sleep and rest."

"I'm thirsty, Mama. Water, please," Wolfgang called to her feebly.

With alarm, Anna Maria saw how feverish Wolfgang had become. His face was flushed, and as he drank he winced, saying, "Even my teeth hurt."

With terror in her heart, Anna Maria realized that this time her cherished son was very ill.

7

Salzburg

Leopold had to send messages to the aristocrats refusing their invitations and explaining that unfortunately his son was not well enough to play at present. The Countess Zinzendorff came to inquire about Wolfgang; when she learned that his parents did not know the cause of his illness, she said, "Please permit me to send my doctor to see what he can do for the child."

The doctor came and examined Wolfgang carefully, then turned to the anxious parents and said, "I fear your little boy will be ill for some time."

"What is it, doctor?" asked Anna Maria fearfully.

"The child has scarlet fever. He will need good care. I cannot stop the course of the disease; see to it that your daughter does not come near him, or she too will get the disease. I am sorry; there is nothing more I can do or say."

Wolfgang lay in bed burning with fever. A red rash covered him from head to toe. His slight body became even thinner. All music had come to a stop, not only for him, but also for Nannerl.

She was not permitted to practice even on the clavichord, despite its dainty sound; nothing was to disturb Wolfgang.

Leopold grew as anxious about his wife's increasing exhaustion as about Wolfgang's illness. He persuaded her to let him relieve her so she would get some sleep; she had been spending almost every moment, night and day, giving her son things to drink, wiping his feverish forehead with cool cloths, freshening his damp pillows; doing anything she could think of to make him more comfortable.

Leopold took his place beside Wolfgang, his eyes fixed on his ailing son's pale face. He patted his limp little hand, murmuring prayers for his recovery.

Because of the contagious disease, their new friends and acquaintances did not dare call on them. Instead they sent notes of encouragement to show they were thinking of them, and sent presents of medicines which were of no use whatever.

Leopold told Anna Maria, "It is kind of our friends to send notes and medicine, but what we need desperately is money. The expense of staying in Vienna is mounting, without any hope now of earning something from the children's concerts. As soon as Wolfgang is no longer contagious and is strong enough to be dressed, we had better return to Salzburg."

"Yes, home is best for him now. Besides, you have overstayed your leave of absence; the Archbishop may be angry and give your position to someone else. Your pay there is small enough, but it is regular and is something we can count on. Whatever we get from the concert tours depends entirely on the whim and fancy of the patrons the children play for. Let us leave as soon as possible."

As soon as Wolfgang was able to sit up in a chair for a little while each day, Leopold began preparing for the long trip back to Salzburg. Early one morning, Wolfgang was dressed warmly, wrapped in a thick blanket, and carried into the carriage.

This time Wolfgang was not well enough to enjoy the journey home in the lumbering coach. Its iron bound wheels clattering over the rough roads made his head ache. No longer were there stops on the way to play for interested bishops and princes. The bumps in the rough roads as the carriage rolled on and on shook Wolfgang's thin body, and he leaned against his mother wearily.

How happy the Salzburg friends were to see the Mozarts home again! But when they saw how frail and exhausted Wolfgang looked, some whispered, "The father is selfishly exploiting his children. Shame!"

Now that the family was unpacked and settled in their own four rooms with Bimperl and Herr Canary, who had been taken care of by neighbors in their absence, friends came often to see them. They saw that Leopold was disappointed that the trip had had to be cut short.

Hagenauer came upstairs to see them and said, "I can't tell you how wonderful it is to have you all back! It was too bad that you had to leave Vienna because of Wolfgang's illness; but even so the journey must have been well justified. I hear that everyone who heard Wolfgang and Nannerl play was greatly impressed. One day you will have to return and continue your successes there."

"I hope so," said Leopold.

While Wolfgang was convalescing, he said, "Papa, would you like to hear the minuet I composed while I was ill?"

"I should say so! Do you feel strong enough to play it for me?"

"Oh, yes. By the way, Papa, have you noticed that Herr Canary always sings and whistles in the key of A? He has a perfect ear and never sings out of tune." Wolfgang laughed happily at the idea.

"He's very much like you in that," said his father lovingly.

Wolfgang played him the minuet, and Leopold was so pleased that he put it down at once into the children's music notebook.

Now that Leopold saw Wolfgang sitting at the harpsichord and clavichord more and more each day, he knew his son was feeling better. He could resume his music lessons with him, and high time, too!

The teaching now became more serious, the hours of instruction longer, interrupted only by Leopold's court duties. Not only were there lessons in playing the keyboard instruments and the violin, but in harmony as well. "If you are to become a composer, it is necessary that you know the grammar of music thoroughly," Leopold told Wolfgang.

In addition to music, Leopold was also teaching Wolfgang and Nannerl reading, writing, and arithmetic. "Geography," he told them, "you will learn through traveling. It is the best possible way to learn such a subject."

Wondering why he and his sister did not, like the other children in the neighborhood, go to school, Wolfgang asked, "Papa, did you go to school when you were a boy?"

"Yes, and I also went to the University of Salzburg. That is why I am qualified to teach you and Nannerl at home instead of sending you to school. In this way you both have much more time for your musical studies. Later on I shall teach you Italian and French; it is very important to be able to speak the languages of the countries we shall be visiting some day."

From time to time Anna Maria asked Leopold, "How are the children getting on in their studies?"

"Very well indeed, Anna Maria. I am greatly encouraged by the pleasure and ease with which they carry out the assignments I give them. I am more and more convinced that their musical education is my sacred task."

A few months later Leopold was making plans for another trip. When he had worked out all of the details of the journey, he announced to his family at supper, "I have good news for all of you. Before long we shall be going on another journey."

Anna Maria's face fell. She was in no hurry to leave home

again. But Wolfgang, already a seasoned traveler, exclaimed, "Hooray! It will be much more fun to go to far-off places than to stay here. Won't it, Nannerl?"

On July ninth the family set forth in their new black lacquered carriage, its doors adorned with skillfully painted floral designs. Leopold expected to be in Munich by the next evening at the latest. He hoped to renew the friendships they had made when he had first taken his children there without Anna Maria, and was looking forward to it keenly.

The carriage, drawn by three fine horses, rolled along a level road that gradually began sloping downhill through a smiling landscape which soon lost itself in the distant hills. Wolfgang and Nannerl peered through the windows with delight, pointing out to one another anything that was especially beautiful or interesting.

They arrived at Wasserburg, on the Inn River. Suddenly there was an explosive crack under their carriage. The children and their parents fell into a heap against each other.

Leopold shouted, "Postilion, what has happened?"

"I'm very sorry, sir," the man called down, "but a wheel has broken. The ruts in the road are terrible. I'm afraid we'll not be able to reach Munich tonight. I shall do my best to find someone to help repair the damage as quickly as possible."

Always ready to make the best of any circumstance or emergency, Wolfgang tried to console his father by saying, "Never mind, Papa, this looks like a very pretty place. Let's stroll about the town. There might be a good organ in that beautiful church over there."

63

"That's not a bad way to pass the time," agreed Leopold.

They all went into the empty church and climbed the steep flight of stairs to the organ-loft. When Wolfgang saw the beautiful organ with carved wooden angels hovering over it, he begged, "Oh, may I try it, Papa?"

"Your legs are much too short to reach the foot pedals, but climb up on the organ bench and I'll show you some things about the instrument. With its organ stops, it can speak with many voices. Nannerl, you go in back and work the bellows so the organ pipes will fill with air."

Patiently Leopold explained to Wolfgang how the foot pedals were used for the bass notes, how one could play on the two parallel keyboards, or manuals, one hand above the other in order to get certain effects. He told him about the knobs, or stops, attached to the sides of the instrument, and how, if the knob that said "flute" on it were pulled out, the single voice of a melody would sound like a flute; however, if you pulled out several stops at the same time, it could sound as if many instruments in an orchestra were playing together.

Wolfgang seemed to understand everything easily and could hardly wait to begin. Leopold went to sit nearby, waiting for Wolfgang to amuse himself while the carriage was being repaired; Nannerl was busily pumping the bellows. All at once he saw Wolfgang push back the organ bench and stand up on the foot pedals because he could not reach them otherwise, using the toes and heels of his shoes like an extra pair of hands.

Running up and down the pedals in proper sequence, improvising and embroidering a melody he had just invented, Wolfgang rejoiced to hear the bass notes boom through the church like the deep voices of a men's choir, the high ones as bright as a trumpet.

The sacristan hurried out from the back of the church to see who was flooding the building with such beautiful music. When he saw that it was only a little boy, skipping over the foot pedals as if his feet had wings, his hands flying over the manuals, he crossed himself piously.

He ran out to spread the news of the child who could play the organ with such heavenly skill. Soon some of the townspeople came running to hear the remarkable little boy.

Leopold sat to one side, thinking and waiting patiently for his Wolferl to finish playing. He had always felt that nothing was too much trouble or bother for him where his children were concerned. He was only too glad to indulge them in any way that increased their musical knowledge or satisfied their eager curiosity. Within him were few doubts about what he considered important and good for their development.

Suddenly his thoughts were interrupted by Wolfgang calling out loudly above the tapestry of sound he was weaving, "Papa! This organ certainly has good lungs!"

Heidelberg

8

June in the year 1763 was particularly beautiful. As the Mozarts rode through southern Germany, not far from Augsburg where Leopold was born, he pointed out, like a guide, palaces and historic buildings they passed, explaining that many were built in French style. There were elaborate gardens imitating the grounds at the French royal palace at Versailles, outdoor marble staircases, and many fountains and ponds on the large estates.

After long hours in the carriage, they finally reached the old university town of Heidelberg. "I think this will be a good place for the children to stretch their legs," Leopold told Anna Maria. "We can climb about the ruins of the castle overlooking the city."

"Then can we go to the Church of the Holy Spirit and try their famous organ, Papa?" asked Wolfgang.

"Certainly, let's do that first."

When the Dean of the church heard Wolfgang play he declared, "This is a historic occasion, and I shall have a plaque put on the organ to say that Wolfgang Amadeus Mozart played on our organ on this date."

When they arrived in Schwetzingen, nearby, where the Prince Elector of Mannheim had his summer palace, Leopold said, "They say the Prince's orchestra is the best in all of Germany. Small wonder, when from every country in Europe he has brought the best musicians he could find. He certainly intends to make his court a center of learning, art, and music; and since he has good taste, a good mind, and great riches, he will undoubtedly accomplish his purpose."

"Perhaps we could play for him, Papa," said Wolfgang.

"I will see what can be done about it," said Leopold.

Leopold managed to let the Prince learn that he was there with his two remarkable children, and in a few days an invitation came. It was not an invitation for the Mozart children to play, but to be present at a concert.

"Even though it is not the kind of invitation we hoped for, it is better than nothing," said their father. "After all, it is an honor to be asked to attend a court concert. Now we can find out for ourselves how good the Prince's musicians are."

It was at this concert that they heard the celebrated Italian violinist, Nardini, who was one of the court musicians. Wolfgang was so overwhelmed by Nardini's playing that he whispered to his father, "I wish I could play like that. How he sings on his violin!"

When the concert was over, the Prince Elector asked Leopold, "Would your children like to play for us?"

"Your Royal Highness, it would be their greatest pleasure."

Inspired by the wonderful musicians who had preceded them, Wolfgang and Nannerl surpassed themselves. The audience of nobles and musicians urged them to play again and again. Leopold and Anna Maria were bursting with pride. If only the Prince would ask Leopold to be one of his court musicians! These were exactly the right surroundings for their son to grow up in. Here his ability would be appreciated, and he would hear outstanding musicians to inspire him. But unfortunately there was no vacancy.

Wolfgang was excited and stimulated by everything he saw and heard. He enjoyed learning and seeing new things, new places, new people. Leopold was determined to keep his children from growing lazy, and he did not relax any of their lessons even during the journey. He told them, "You both have keen musical ears, so it should be easy for you to learn new languages. Be sure to practice your French on each other constantly." Wolfgang delighted in calling his sister *Mademoiselle* at every opportunity.

By August the Mozart family was in Frankfurt. Leopold had arranged in advance that his children should give a concert there.

Anna Maria was glad to see that Nannerl was as highly appreciated as Wolfgang at this court, for she considered her daughter just as talented as her son. It would have pained her to see Nannerl's feelings hurt, or to have her children become envious of each other's success.

But there was no need for her to worry. Wolfgang loved and admired Nannerl so much that he was always happiest when she was praised more than he was.

Among those who came to hear Wolfgang and Nannerl play in Frankfurt was young Goethe, fourteen years old at the time. When he became a famous poet and writer, he said that in all his life he never forgot how he felt about the little boy and his sister.

Greatly encouraged by the success of the concert, Leopold inserted a notice in the Frankfurt newspaper saying:

"The unanimous admiration of the public and the great interest taken in the exceptionally talented children of Mr. Leopold Mozart, composer, conductor, and violinist to his Most Serene Highness, the Prince Archbishop of Salzburg, has induced him to permit them to give three more concerts.

"The little girl, in her twelfth year, and the boy, almost seven, will play the most difficult works of the great masters. Not only will the boy play on the harpsichord, but he will perform a violin concerto as well. Furthermore, accompanied by an orchestra, he will pay the harpsichord whose keys will be covered by a cloth just as easily as if they were uncovered. He will also play and improvise on the organ on any theme submitted, no matter how difficult. This will prove his skill on this particular instrument, so different from the harpsichord."

70

Leopold was becoming a clever concert manager. He pointed out to Anna Maria, "It is important for our son's future that we make the most of every opportunity. One day he will surely be engaged as court composer and musician to some great prince who will not underestimate him."

After a great success in Frankfurt, the Mozarts set out again. At the Rhine they left their carriage to continue their journey in a small boat. Wolfgang and Nannerl were enchanted by the other boats that passed them, the charming little villages along the banks, the glimpses of ruined castles perched on hilltops.

At Cologne they left the boat and were met by their carriage, which proceeded to Aix-la-Chapelle. There the Princess Amalie, sister of King Frederick the Great of Prussia, invited them to come and play for her. She herself was a trained musician and an ardent lover of music. When she heard Wolfgang and Nannerl play, her enthusiasm knew no bounds.

"You must take your children to Berlin to play for my brother," she told Leopold. "He loves music and plays the flute delightfully."

"It would be a great honor, indeed, Your Highness, but we can no longer put off going to Paris and London. Some other time the children will gladly play for His Majesty," said Leopold.

"How adored and admired your children must be by the fortunate Elector of Salzburg!" said the Princess.

Tactfully Leopold replied, "Your Highness, a musician often has to make his reputation elsewhere before he is appreciated at home. Nowadays, unless a musician is taught by Italian or French

71

teachers, he is not valued highly, as I am sure you understand."

"I understand perfectly. But do come back with your lovely children," she said, embracing Wolfgang and Nannerl warmly.

For all her enthusiasm and kind words, there was no present for the children's playing, and Leopold was deeply disappointed. He wrote home to his landlord, Hagenauer, "If each of the Princess's kisses had been a gold piece, we would have had plenty with which to pay both our hotel and coach bill."

The journey was costly; sometimes Leopold was as anxious as Anna Maria about their increasing expenses. Before they were noticed or received by the nobles in important new towns and cities, Leopold often had to wait and wait for their invitations. In the meantime, their living expenses soared.

Mostly the presents received consisted of watches, jewels, clothes, candy, tiny swords for Wolfgang, laces for Nannerl. If only people would give money instead, thought Leopold.

"What in the world are we going to do with all these things, Papa?" asked Nannerl.

"Open a shop and sell them!" said Wolfgang merrily.

They reached Brussels and waited three weeks for the Prince, who had promised to hear Wolfgang and Nannerl; then they found that he was too busy hunting, eating, and drinking to have time for the Mozart family. Regretfully, they set forth for Paris by way of Liège. They liked Belgium, marvelling at the lovely churches, convents, and castles they passed on the way to France.

All at once Wolfgang took a fancy to calling himself "His Majesty," and he insisted on being referred to by his self-appointed title. He amused his parents and Nannerl by giving fantastic and humorous names to the towns and rivers they passed and inventing extraordinary stories of his domain. He said to them, after he had been busily scrawling something, "Here is a map I am making of my estates along the way."

At last they arrived in Paris. Wolfgang and Nannerl were tremendously excited to see the famous city, to hear the people speaking the language they were now learning. Turning to Nannerl, Wolfgang said, "Mademoiselle, are you clever enough to understand what the people on the street are saying?"

"And how about you, Monsieur?" she responded.

"Mama, just look at the splendid buildings and gardens and statues. They are much grander than anything we have seen," said Wolfgang.

"This must be a very rich country," observed Nannerl. "Who is the king, Papa?"

"King Louis XV, and he has one of the most luxurious courts in all of Europe. They say, though, that the people are very poor and miserable."

"Dear me, just see those ragged beggars!" said Wolfgang, full of pity.

"Oh, Mama, did you see those painted ladies, just like dolls!" cried Nannerl.

"They are disgusting," said Anna Maria firmly. "And how filthy the streets are — ugh!"

"Don't worry about the dirty streets, my dear," said Leopold. "I will hire sedan chairs for you and the children, and strong men to carry you about in them." Then he said to Wolfgang and Nannerl, "From now on, remember you must speak only French to one another. Then you will find it easy to say anything you wish. Take my advice, use the language of the country you are in."

Apprehensive as usual, Anna Maria asked Leopold, "How are we going to get acquainted with people in such a big city?"

"First I shall put a notice in the newspaper announcing the arrival of our children and describing what they are able to do. It will surely arouse interest, and word will spread around."

Wolfgang and Nannerl were not worried about anything. Their clever Papa knew how to manage everything!

Paris

9

The newspaper notice had good results. A compatriot of Leopold's, Grimm, who was secretary to the Duke of Orleans in Paris, came to see him. He had high standing as a musical connoisseur and was a well-known figure in Parisian society, so that he was able to spread word about the astonishing Mozart children where it would do the most good. He was charmed as soon as he saw them and heard them play, and immediately became their sponsor.

In addition, the wife of the Bavarian ambassador to France, who was a native of Salzburg, invited Leopold and his family to be her house guests at the German Embassy. This was not only a great convenience but a saving. Besides, she promised to obtain an invitation for the children to play at the palace of Versailles.

Grimm was very helpful, telling people about Wolfgang and Nannerl enthusiastically and trying to get them engagements to play. Secretly he had Wolfgang's first harpsichord sonatas engraved and brought them to him as a present, saying, "I want everyone to see and play what you were able to compose at the age of seven."

While the Mozart family was waiting for the longed-for royal invitation, Grimm obtained a letter from Prince de Conti inviting Wolfgang and Nannerl to play for him. There Wolfgang met the Prince's composer and orchestra conductor, Johann Schobert. He composed chamber music; Wolfgang had an opportunity to study Schobert's work. Later this had an influence on some of Wolfgang's compositions.

Days and weeks went by, and still no royal invitation arrived. Leopold began to despair. In a few days it would be Christmas. He did not feel at all cheerful about their lack of success in Paris thus far.

After a month of impatient waiting, the King's invitation finally came. The Mozarts were invited to come to Versailles for two weeks.

"This is even better than I had hoped!" exclaimed Leopold jubilantly.

The splendor and lavishness of the court at Versailles exceeded anything they had imagined. The famous gardens, the fountains spraying water high into the air, the richly brocaded garments of the ladies and gentlemen with their valuable jewels, the extraordinary height and elaborateness of the women's pow-

76

dered headdresses, left the Mozart family speechless.

The first night, when they were going to bed, Wolfgang said to Nannerl, "Mademoiselle, can you believe that we are actually living in the same palace as the King of France?"

"Pinch me, Wolfgang, so I'll know I'm not dreaming," said Nannerl. "What a relief it is not to have to bow and bend the knee. Mr. Grimm says it is considered bad taste to do so here, and that the gentlemen are not supposed to do more than lift their hat to the King and Queen."

Wolfgang and Nannerl were summoned to play for the King in his own apartment. On another day they were asked to play for the Queen in hers. They were especially pleased when they saw the Queen's three little daughters and her grandson, the little Dauphin, were present. The grandson was later to become the husband of Marie Antoinette, the little girl who had helped Wolfgang when he fell down at Schönbrunn.

On New Year's day Leopold was informed that he and his family were invited to be present at the royal dinner. In anticipation of the feast, Wolfgang began rubbing his tummy until Leopold informed him, "It's not an invitation to eat, only to be *present*."

"Not to eat!" exclaimed Wolfgang and Nannerl in dismay.

They entered the vast, beautiful dining room and found it so cold that they began to shiver. Wolfgang and Nannerl were given the privilege of standing behind the King and Queen, their backs to the huge fireplace in which enormous logs burned. The Queen, who was Polish, spoke to Wolfgang in German; from

time to time she fed him bits from her plate.

Wolfgang's back felt as if it were roasting. The fire was roaring behind him in a fireplace high enough for a tall man to stand in. A short distance away from it, it was so cold that it made Wolfgang realize why everyone was dressed in furs. Perhaps the wine at the other end of the table was frozen!

He remembered how cozy and warm their dining room in Salzburg was, heated by a tall blue-tiled stove. His father had often commented on the inefficient manner of heating the vast palace by means of open fireplaces. There were servants who did nothing but attend to the fires, carrying heavy logs to feed the devouring flames.

When the two weeks were over, Leopold was delighted to find how generous the King and Queen were, as well as the nobles at whose houses Wolfgang and Nannerl had often played. The children had been presented with what amounted to several hundred dollars, and overwhelmed with praise.

For Wolfgang and Nannerl, the two weeks at Versailles had been especially exciting. Wolfgang had had an opportunity to hear French music and French opera, which he found very different from the kind of music he had heard elsewhere.

He told his father, "I like French music. It has elegance and delicacy. I wish I could write music like that."

After five months in Paris, Leopold announced to his family one April day, "It is time for us to go on to London."

Anna Maria looked very pleased. She had disliked the mud and filth of Paris, and had been disgusted by the painted, immodest women, and the profligacy of the court.

Because the regular packet ship was full, the Mozart family had to cross over from Calais to England in a smaller ship. Wolfgang, Nannerl, and Anna Maria became so seasick that they thought their end was near. When their boat reached England, they were so dizzy and miserable they could hardly stand. Leopold, however, was in fine spirits, and tried to cheer them by saying, "Well, my dears, I have a pocket full of valuable introductions to people in London. I am sure that the Queen, who is German and very musical, will be inviting you to come and play for her and the King."

"I have been told that the King likes only food and hunting," said Anna Maria pessimistically.

"And music, Mama!" declared Wolfgang, defending him. "Papa said King George of England was the great patron of Handel. I hope we can meet Handel."

"I am sorry to disappoint you, Wolfgang, but Handel died five years ago," said Leopold. "The year before the present King George came to the throne. It was his great grandfather and his grandfather, George I and George II, who were Handel's patrons, not George III."

"That was, let me see — 1759," said Wolfgang, always fond of arithmetic. "I was three years old then, wasn't I? Papa, why didn't we come here then? Why did you wait so long?"

Leopold chuckled and said, "Although Handel is no longer alive you will hear plenty of his music in England. Everyone here loves his music, and it is played constantly."

In London the Mozart family did not have to wait as long as in Paris for a royal invitation to play at the palace. When they were taken to see the King and Queen, the warmth and friendliness of the royal couple won them over completely. Queen Charlotte's passion for music filled St. James's Palace with beautiful sounds.

Leopold wrote to Lorenz Hagenauer:

"On April 27 we were from six to nine o'clock with the King and Queen in St. James's Palace. The present was only 24 guineas but the favor with which His Majesty and Queen showered us is not to be described. One would never, in short, think that these friendly people were King and Queen of England — the way we have been received here surpasses everything. Eight days later we were walking in St. James's Park. The King and Queen drove past, and although we were in other clothes, they recognized us. The King opened the window, nodded, and smilingly greeted us, especially Wolfgang.

"On May 19 we were brought to court and were from six to ten o'clock with the King and Queen. The King put before Wolfgang pieces by Wagenseil, Christian Bach, Abel, and Handel. He has played them all at sight. He played on the King's organ in such a way that they even preferred it to his harpsichord playing. He accompanied the Queen in a song, and a flutist in a solo. Finally he took the bass of a Handel aria and improvised a most beautiful melody on it to the astonishment of all. In a word, what he knew when we started from Salzburg is a mere shadow of what he knows now. It surpasses all imagination."

With gifts of money from the King and with what came from outside concerts, Leopold was able to send Hagenauer a large payment toward his debt. How glad Anna Maria was to be able partly to repay their benefactor at home!

Suddenly Leopold caught a severe chill after an outdoor charity concert where Wolfgang played. He became so ill that their doctor advised the family to move to Chelsea, a short distance outside London, where it was more quiet and more countrylike.

Anna Maria told Wolfgang and Nannerl, "You mustn't practice or make any noise that will disturb your sick father."

Composing music made no noise, and as Wolfgang had no lack of tunes running about in his head, he decided to put his musical ideas down on paper. He would write a symphony, but secretly, as a surprise for his father. While he was working at it, Nannerl came to sit beside him. "What are you doing, Wolfgang?"

"Writing a symphony."

"Really?"

"Yes, and please remind me to give the horns plenty to do."

"I thought you didn't like the sound of horns," said Nannerl. "When you were smaller, you used to get so pale when you heard the blasting noise of a horn that you would cover your ears and almost fall into a faint."

"Oh, that was long ago, when I was a little boy. Now, I'm eight, and I know that horns are very important in a symphony — that is, if you know how to make them behave."

London

It was several weeks before Leopold was himself again. The day he was able to get out of bed, Wolfgang said, "I have a present for you, Papa." From behind him he drew a sheaf of music and handed it to his father.

Leopold read on the title page, *Symphony No. I in E flat Major*.

"A symphony!" exclaimed Leopold.

"And I have ideas for two more, Papa," said Wolfgang.

"That is good news, my son. You will have plenty of time for composing and playing because I am planning for us to stay on in London. The English are a very special nation, and it is a pleasure to be with them. It will give you an opportunity to hear Handel's wonderful operas and oratorios and be with excellent composers and musicians."

"I am so glad we shall stay, Papa, because I just love the Queen's music teacher. Is Johann Christian Bach very old?"

"Goodness, no. He is only 29 years old, the youngest son of the great master, Johann Sebastian Bach. Everyone calls Johann Christian the 'English Bach' to distinguish him from his famous father. I hope you realize that he does you the honor of treating you as if you were a grown musician instead of a boy of eight," said Leopold.

"Yes, it is nice of him, Papa. What fun it was when he started a fugue on the harpsichord and asked me to continue it. Then do you remember the way he had us play a sonata together behind a screen, each of us taking turns every few bars, and asking the listeners to guess which one of us was playing? It was certainly easy to fool them."

During the summer months Wolfgang composed the two other symphonies, and he wrote down in his sketch book smaller compositions to be worked on later.

A few months later Leopold arranged a concert in which Wolfgang's first symphonies were performed. He also had the six violin sonatas Wolfgang had been composing printed and dedicated to Queen Charlotte. It was a way of thanking her for her patronage, and, Leopold hoped, of stimulating her to continue her generosity. For this Leopold was presented with 50 guineas, over two hundred and fifty dollars.

Wolfgang and Nannerl were soon invited to play again at the palace in honor of the fourth anniversary of the King's accession to the throne.

In London the fantastic stories and reports of Wolfgang's unusual musical ability aroused the suspicions of an English gentleman, the Honorable Daines Barrington. He decided to find out for himself if what was said about this musical child from Austria was true.

The doubting Englishman even wrote to the church registry in Salzburg to obtain the dates of Wolfgang's and Nannerl's births. The exacting tests to which he put Wolfgang convinced Barrington that Leopold had not exaggerated about his ability. He drew up a full report of his findings for a scientific journal in which he said:

"I carried Wolfgang Amadeus Mozart a manuscript duet composed by an English gentleman. The whole score was in five parts. My intention was to hear incontestable proof of Wolfgang's abilities as a player at sight, it being absolutely impossible that he could ever have seen the music before.

"The score was no sooner put upon his desk than he began to play the symphony in a most masterly manner, as well as in the time and style which corresponded with the intention of the composer. I mention this circumstance because the greatest masters often fail in these particulars on the first trial.

"His voice, in the tone of it, was thin and infantile, but nothing could exceed the masterly manner in which he sang.

"His father, who performed the underpart in this duet, was once or twice out, though the passages were not more difficult than those in the upper one; on which occasions the son looked back with some anger, pointing out to him some mistakes and setting him right.

"His execution was amazing, considering that his little fingers could scarce reach a sixth on the harpsichord. His astonishing readiness, however, did not rise merely from great practice; he had a thorough knowledge of the fundamentals of composition. He was also a great master of modulation and his transitions from one key to another were exceedingly natural and judicious.

"Witness as I was myself, I must own that I could not help suspecting his father imposed, with regard to the real age of the boy, though he had only a most childish appearance, but likewise had all the actions of that stage of life.

"For example, while he was playing to me, a favorite cat came in, upon which he immediately left his harpsichord, nor could we bring him back for a considerable time.

"He would also sometimes run about the room with a stick between his legs by way of a horse."

Wolfgang had thoroughly convinced the Honorable Daines that he *was* an eight-year-old marvel.

It delighted Wolfgang to find he could hear many Italian operas in London. He found them very humorous compared to the French ones, and Leopold took him to hear them often, thinking they might have a great influence on him. In this way, Wolfgang was able to hear some of the greatest Italian singers and to become acquainted with the work of Italian composers.

One of the most famous of the singers was Manzuoli. When the singer was introduced to Wolfgang, whose fame had already reached him, Manzuoli offered to give the boy free singing lessons. Leopold was delighted to let his son accept, for this training would give Wolfgang some knowledge of how to write for voices. This knowledge was to stand him in good stead later when he began to compose operas.

Leopold had hoped they would be invited to play for the King again, but there was serious trouble with the American colonies, and George III was not in good health.

Now Leopold began advertising in London papers that his children would give public concerts. Every day, from noon to three in the afternoon, Leopold held open house. For a small sum, visitors were invited to hear Wolfgang and Nannerl perform. Once they even played in a tavern.

"Appreciation and praise of our children are all well enough," Leopold told Anna Maria, "but it is money that pays for food and lodging."

One July day Leopold said, "There is nothing more to be gained by remaining in London, Anna Maria. The King is too busy with his troubles, and the public seems to be tired of our children. But I do not despair: there are still new worlds to conquer. We have invitations from Holland. The sister of the Prince of Orange at The Hague wishes to hear the children play."

Anna Maria packed their clothes, Leopold gathered up their musical instruments, and they said good-by to their English friends.

When they reached The Hague, Nannerl was not feeling well, so Wolfgang played alone.

Suddenly Nannerl grew desperately ill, so ill indeed that Leopold and Anna Maria were sure she would die, and the doctor lost all hope. She was so weak she could hardly speak, but when she did, Leopold wrote Hagenauer, "In her sleep she talked

English, French, and German in such a way that in spite of our trouble we had to laugh."

Soon after this, Wolfgang became as sick as Nannerl. "After he was out of danger," wrote Leopold to his friend, "he slept for almost eight days and never spoke until at last his strength returned; then he spoke day and night, but quite unintelligibly."

The doctor told Leopold, "Your children have been exhausted by their busy irregular life. It is too full of excitement and change."

At this Anna Maria looked at Leopold with reproach in her eyes.

With her tender and careful nursing the children finally recovered, but Wolfgang was a shadow of himself. When he was able to sit up he asked for pencil and paper, and composed a symphony in Italian style.

"I must have been thinking about all those beautiful Italian operas I heard in London, Papa," he said.

Wolfgang and Nannerl grew stronger and again began giving concerts in The Hague. Here too they were a great success. Wolfgang dedicated his most recent violin sonatas to the princess, and Leopold gave a Dutch translation of his "Violin Method" to the prince.

Well pleased with the financial returns in Holland, Leopold and his family left for Switzerland, where Wolfgang and Nannerl gave nine concerts. In May they returned to Paris. Again they were invited to play at Versailles, and now Wolfgang wrote a religious composition for voices, with string accompaniment.

Leopold reported to Hagenauer:

"God has given to my children such talents as to incite me, apart from the obligations of a father, to devote everything to their good education. Every moment that I lose is lost forever, and if ever I realized how invaluable time is for the young, it is now. You know that my children are accustomed to work. Should they become used to idleness my whole edifice is overthrown. Habit is an iron shirt, and you yourself know how much my children, especially Wolfgang, have to learn. Who knows what our return to Salzburg brings? Perhaps we shall be received in such a way that we shall gladly take up our pack and set off again. If they are not wanted, I am not to blame."

In Munich, Wolfgang fell ill again. Worried, Anna Maria said, "Leopold, let us go home before our precious son's health is destroyed by these three years of journeying and performing."

As soon as Wolfgang had recovered sufficiently, they returned to Salzburg. Wolfgang was now ten years old. He had visited southern Germany, France, Belgium, Holland, Switzerland, and England. He had met and played for famous musicians and composers, had been taken to the opera and to churches, and had heard and composed much music.

Wolfgang said, "If I had been sent to school like other children, Papa, I would not have learned and seen as much in three years as I have."

"It is true, my son, and I believe you have absorbed a great deal of the music you have heard. It will have a good effect on your own music, though I hope your compositions will not be an imitation of the others."

Later Leopold told his wife, "There is no single influence I can recognize in Wolfgang's music. He is like a butterfly which flits from flower to flower, gathering something from each one. He is just beginning to discover what lies within him."

Milan

Upon their return to Salzburg, friends complimented Leopold. "Your son has returned a master musician. You have done well by him."

Leopold did not slacken work on his children's education. He was constantly setting Wolfgang musical problems for him to solve in his notebook. The Archbishop asked Wolfgang to write several religious cantatas, a symphony, instrumental music to be played outdoors, minuets, marches, fanfares for trumpets and kettle drums.

Ten months later, in September, 1767, Leopold and his family set out again for Vienna to attend the festivities in connection with the approaching marriage of Josepha, daughter of the Empress Maria Theresa, to the King of Naples.

"It will be an excellent opportunity to make our children's talents known again, Anna Maria," said Leopold.

But hardly had they arrived in Vienna when an epidemic of smallpox broke out. The bride-to-be caught the disease, and therefore Wolfgang was not yet asked to play at court. It was suggested to Leopold that he have his children inoculated, but he refused to take the risk. "I prefer to leave it all in God's hands," he said. "Let Him in His divine mercy dispose as He will of the life of this wonder of nature."

But when the Princess Josepha died, Leopold grew frightened and took his loved ones away from Vienna to Olmütz. Alas, it was too late. First Wolfgang came down with the dread disease, then Nannerl. They had such poor living quarters that Leopold went to Count Podatsky, the Dean of the cathedral at Olmütz, to tell him of their plight. Immediately he gave them rooms in his small palace, where the Mozart family remained for two months.

When the children recovered and the Mozarts returned to Vienna, they received an invitation from the saddened Empress, a widow as well as a bereaved mother, for the Emperor Francis had died in 1765. Her son Joseph was the new Emperor. Leopold wrote home:

"You cannot imagine with what kindness the Empress spoke with my wife about the children's illness and our great tour, pressing her hand and stroking her cheeks compassionately, while the Emperor Joseph spoke with me about musical and other matters and made Nannerl blush often. You must not conclude from this affability that we shall get an exceptional present."

92

Since her husband's and daughter's deaths the Empress no longer gave musical parties; whatever musical commissions were given now depended on her frugal son. There were many nobles at court who thought only of balls, masquerades, and dances.

Now that Wolfgang was twelve years old, he was becoming a serious rival, a threat to established musicians, many of whom always feared losing their positions to someone better. Instead of his powers waning, as those of most musical prodigies do, they were increasing. And now the jealous musicians learned that the Emperor had asked Wolfgang if he would like to compose a comic opera!

"I should be delighted at the opportunity, Your Highness!" said Wolfgang, and immediately set to work, using the play of an Italian theatrical poet for the plot. He called the opera, *The Pretended Simpleton.* But even before it was finished, intrigues began to keep the opera from being produced.

First the theater manager told Leopold, "The opera house, alas, will not be available, since there are other concerts that must come before your son's opera."

After that, the orchestra musicians said, "We refuse to be conducted by a child." Some said, even before hearing the opera, "The music won't be worth anything, because the boy doesn't know Italian well enough to match the play to the music." Others declared, "Anyway, it is the father, not the son, who has written the composition."

Leopold was furious! He decided he would convince them at any cost, even if he had to go directly to the Emperor with his complaints. But despite anything he could do, the opera was not performed. Dr. Mesmer, a wealthy doctor and the discoverer of hypnosis, knew the Mozarts, and decided to console them in their frustrations and disappointments by commissioning Wolfgang to write a short opera that could be performed in a large room in his house. Wolfgang immediately composed *Bastien and Bastienne,* which was greatly enjoyed by the audience and the proud doctor.

Another acquaintance commissioned a Mass, to be sung at the dedication of a new chapel in an orphan asylum, famous for its excellent instruction in music. The Emperor came with his sisters and brothers to hear the orphans sing Wolfgang's composition with Wolfgang conducting it. Everyone was greatly impressed by the beauty of the music.

It was soon after this that the Mozarts returned to Salzburg. The Archbishop had heard about *The Pretended Simpleton,* and he asked that the opera be performed in his palace. After hearing it, the Archbishop appointed Wolfgang one of his court musicians. But being a musician in Salzburg was not very stimulating for Wolfgang, and toward the end of the year 1769, when Wolfgang was almost fourteen years old, he and his father left for a tour of Italy. This time Anna Maria and Nannerl were left at home.

In the eighteenth century, Italy was considered the source of fine music by musicians. Not only did music flourish in the princely courts in all the important cities, but in addition there were rich monasteries and churches that were famous for the composing and teaching of music.

On the way to Italy, Wolfgang said to his father, "Didn't Handel and Johann Christian Bach study in Italy?"

"Yes, they did. You can see why I think you should do so, too, my son."

On the way, Wolfgang wrote to Anna Maria:

"Dearest Mother, My heart is completely ravished from sheer joy because this journey is so jolly, because it is so warm in the coach and our coachman is a splendid man, who when the road permits goes like the wind. Papa will have written the description of our journey. The reason I have written, Mama, is to show that I know my duty and that I am with the deepest respect your faithful son,

Wolfgang Mozart"

Leopold enclosed a separate letter saying:

"On our arrival in Verona, there was such a crowd that we had scarcely room to get out of the coach. When it was over the uproar was still greater because everyone wanted to see the little organist.

"We have had it very cold for eight days, and imagine! everywhere we eat there is neither a stove nor heating in the dining room. One's hands get blue with cold."

From Milan, a week later, he continued:

"Thank God I left you at home. Firstly you would not have stood the cold, secondly it would have cost a terrible lot, for we should not have had the choice of lodging we now have, in the Augustine Monastery where, although we pay, we are better off and more comfortable. Every night our beds are warmed so that Wolfgang at bedtime is always happy.

"At Mantua Wolfgang gave a concert of his compositions and also improvised so remarkably that people referred to him as a wonder-work of Nature. The calls, the applause, uproar and bravos, in short the general admiration, is not to be described, but we shall not become rich. It is enough if we pay our traveling expenses."

To Nannerl, Wolfgang wrote a letter that was a mixture of German, Italian, French, and English, describing an opera he heard. He said, however, ". . . there is such a noise in the theater one can hear nothing, for Italian audiences can not restrain their audible comments and conversation."

In Milan Wolfgang was commissioned to write another opera, and he set to work on it eagerly.

The letters that came from Anna Maria often showed her concern for her precious son's health. Leopold wrote assuring her, "Wolfgang is fat and healthy, and the whole day long he is lively and gay."

To which Wolfgang added a postscript to Nannerl. "Mariandel, I am so glad you have been so terrifically jolly. Addio . . . farewell. I kiss Mama's hand a thousand times, and to you I send one hundred loving smacks or pats on your wonderful horse-face."

On their way from Milan to Parma, Wolfgang composed his first string quartet in a single evening. When his father asked, "How could you compose these three movements so quickly?" Wolfgang answered, "Oh, it was easy. They were already completed in my head. All I had to do was to write them down."

In March they arrived in Bologna, and Wolfgang wrote Nannerl:

"As I had been lazy so long I thought there'd be no harm if I again became industrious for a bit. Always on days when the German post comes, the food and drink tastes better to me. Write how the Haydnish minuets please you, and if they are better than the first."

Leopold added a postscript to his wife:

"Wolfgang is more admired here than in any other of the Italian towns, since this is the seat and residence of so many masters, artists, and scholars. He is also most in request, and this increases his fame throughout Italy, since Father Martini is the god of the Italians, and he speaks of Wolfgang with such admiration and has personally tested him."

Rome

I2

During Holy Week Leopold
and Wolfgang went to Rome. Leopold wrote to his wife:

"In Rome they say that they have had rain for four months,
and we truly had an experience of it, for on Wednesday and
Thursday we went, in fine weather, to hear the *Miserere* in the
Sistine Chapel at St. Peter's, and were overtaken by such rain that
our cloaks have never been so soaked. Of the horrible journey here
I shall say little.

"You will perhaps have heard of the celebrated *Miserere* in
Rome, which is so highly treasured that the musicians are forbid-
den under threat of excommunication to let a single part of it be
taken out of the Chapel or to copy it or give it to anyone. *We
alone have it*. Wolfgang has written it down . . . we shall bring it
home with us, and as it is one of the secrets of Rome we will not let it
pass into other hands so as not to incur the direct or indirect displeasure of the Church."

Wolfgang had written out the seventeenth-century composition from memory upon returning to their lodgings after hearing it once on the Wednesday before Good Friday. When it was repeated on Good Friday he took the manuscript with him — hiding it in his hat, he made some corrections. What he had done became known and caused a great sensation. He was called in to produce his copy in the presence of one of the Pope's singers, who was amazed at its correctness.

When Leopold received Anna Maria's letter showing her fright on his account, he wrote immediately.

"There is nothing in the least to be worried about. It is taken quite another way here. All Rome knows of it. The Pope himself knows that Wolfgang has written down the *Miserere*. There is nothing to be afraid of; it has brought him great honor.

"The deeper we penetrate into Italy the greater grows the astonishment. Wolfgang does not stand still but develops so much from day to day that the greatest connoisseurs and masters cannot find words to express their admiration."

Wolfgang composed another symphony and more songs. Often when he wrote home he made up nonsensical rhymes and drew pictures of people and places to amuse his mother and Nannerl. He was always so lively and in such high spirits that his pen flew away with him.

"I am, God be praised and thanked, apart from my miserable pen, well, and kiss Mama and Nannerl a thousand times. I only wish that my sister were in Rome, for this city would surely please her well, since the Peter's Church is the real thing, and so are many things in Rome. Now I have just drawn St. Peter with the keys,

St. Paul with the sword, and St. Luke together with my sister. I have had the honor of kissing St. Peter's foot at St. Peter's, and as I have the misfortune to be so little, they lifted me, your old Wolfgang Mozart, up."

From Rome they went to Naples, traveling in the company of some monks to Naples, because the roads were infested with bandits. Wolfgang was enchanted by the beauty of Naples, with its lovely bay and the volcano, Vesuvius, hovering over it threateningly. He gave some concerts there and heard some Italian operas which delighted him.

In June Leopold wrote to Anna Maria:

"Our concert was very successful. The Princess of Francaville has made us a good present, and we still have a few stray small expectations. You will be vexed that I do not let you know our receipts in detail. I don't give them because in Salzburg they consider only what we get and don't think of the expenses, for very few know what traveling costs. It is enough if I tell you that, God be praised, we lack nothing for our journeys to be made in decent comfort."

So superstitious were the Italians that when Wolfgang was playing at the Naples Conservatory, people in the audience were sure there was magic in the ring Wolfgang wore. They demanded: "Take the ring off and play again!" Of course he played just as well without it as with it; their admiration and wonder were greater than ever, and they redoubled their applause. "I only wish there *were* magic in the ring," said Wolfgang, laughing.

Wolfgang wrote to Nannerl:

100

"Write and tell me how Herr Canary is. Does he still sing? Does he still pipe? Do you know why I think of the canary? Because in our lobby there is one that makes a noise just like ours. . . . Yesterday we put on our new clothes; we looked as beautiful as angels.

"Thank God we are well. I especially, when a letter comes from Salzburg. I beg you to write to me every post, even when you have nothing to write I would like to have it so as to have a letter every post-day. It would not be a bad thing if you write me sometimes a letter in Italian."

A little later he wrote:

"Vesuvius is smoking furiously today. . . . I shall now begin to write an account of my life. I awake at nine o'clock, sometimes not till ten, and then we go out, and then we dine and after dinner we write, and then we take a walk, and afterwards we sup. On a meat-day half a chicken, or a morsel of roast, on a fast-day a little fish; and then we go to sleep. . . . I hope you are well, and likewise Mama. Naples and Rome are two sleepy cities. . . . Write to me and don't be so lazy. Otherwise you will have a beating from me. . . . The King at the opera stands on a foot stool so as to seem taller than the Queen. . . ."

In July the Pope conferred on Wolfgang the Order of the Golden Spur, together with a golden cross to wear. Leopold was immensely pleased and wanted Wolfgang to use his title of "Knight," which he did for a little while just to please his father; since he was too modest to care about it, he soon forgot to use it.

By August Leopold wrote to Anna Maria:

"Wolfgang's clothes are getting too small for him and he has now no singing voice; it has neither high nor low tones. This vexes him very much, for he cannot sing his own things which often he would like to sing to himself."

Returning to Bologna, Wolfgang had the privilege of studying counterpoint with the priest-composer, Father Martini, and wrote several compositions. Although Wolfgang was only fourteen years old, the Bologna Philharmonic Society elected him a member of their distinguished group, after prescribing a difficult test piece to be written in old church modes according to elaborate rules. Leopold wrote home:

"Wolfgang had to appear in the Academy Hall on October 9th at four in the afternoon. Then the head of the Academy and two censors, in the presence of the members, gave him an antiphon from the antiphonary, which he had to set in four parts in a neighboring room into which he was locked. When it was ready it was examined by the censors and all the conductors and composers, who voted on it by means of white and black balls. As all the balls were white, he was called in and everyone clapped and wished him well as he entered and was proclaimed a member. He returned thanks and the ceremony ended. . . . I was on the other side of the hall in the library all the time. Everyone was astonished that he was ready so soon, for many have taken three hours on an antiphon of three lines. You must know that this kind of composition is by no means easy, as many things are excluded. . . . He finished in exactly half an hour."

Wolfgang added a postscript for Nannerl.

"May you live hundreds of years still and die when you are a thousand. I have no time to write more. The pen is not worth a fig, like him who guides it. The title of the opera I have to compose

102

at Milan is not yet known. I have got "The Thousand and One Nights" in Italian as a present from our hostess in Rome. It is most amusing to read.

"My violin now has new strings and I play every day, but I only put this in because Mama asked once if I still played the violin. I have been more than six times alone to churches and functions. I have already composed four Italian symphonies besides arias."

To his mother two weeks later he wrote:

"I am still active and in truth gay. Today the whim took me to ride on a donkey; for it is the custom in Italy, so I thought I must also try it. I cannot write much as my finger hurts through writing so many recitatives. I beg you to pray for me that my opera goes well, and that we can then be once more happy together."

In Milan Wolfgang worked on the opera, *Mitridate,* but again there were intrigues of all kinds, and difficulties with singers. But with patience and tact Leopold and Wolfgang overcame them, and the opera commenced rehearsing for production.

Leopold wrote Anna Maria:

"Our lodging is not far from the theater and consists of a large room with a balcony and three windows. There is a stove in the room. The bedroom is the same size, with two large windows and no stove. The bed is as broad as nine good-sized men.

"We wish you both good health and especially cheaper times as you are always giving me the depressing news that everything gets dearer. Patience! We shall, with God's help, happily bite our way through the unavoidable vexations.

"If our good friends, from time to time, can supply a joke in your letter it will be welcome, for Wolfgang is now so occupied with his opera *Mitridate,* and consequently very serious. I am delighted if something amusing comes his way.

"Before the first rehearsal people declared it impossible that such a young boy, and above all, a German, could write an Italian opera. Since the first rehearsal all these people are dumbfounded."

On June 5, 1771, Leopold wrote again, "Our son's opera continues its success. It was given twenty times."

Afterwards Leopold and Wolfgang went to Venice for the carnival season, where Wolfgang gave a concert to a deeply impressed audience. How Wolfgang loved Venice, with its canals, gondolas, and gay palaces, and St. Mark's Cathedral, the square filled with pigeons! It was hard to leave the beautiful city and its pretty girls and singing boatmen.

"We have to go home now," Leopold told Wolfgang. "We have been away a long time."

"Yes, my fourteenth and fifteenth birthdays were spent far from Mother and Nannerl. I long to see them."

In Salzburg everyone found Wolfgang as modest as before, unspoiled by his successes in Italy. He had brought back with him many new compositions, especially church music. Now he received a commission from the Empress Maria Theresa to compose a theatrical cantata to celebrate the marriage of her son Ferdinand to an Italian princess in October.

"Why, that's only a month away!" exclaimed Wolfgang. "But I can do it easily."

It meant that Wolfgang had to go to Milan again. From there he wrote to Nannerl:

"My dearest Sister!

"We have had to endure great heat on the journey and the dust has parched us so that we should have suffocated and perished had we not been cleverer.

"Above us there is a violinist, beneath us another, close by a singing master is giving a lesson, in the room opposite us is an oboist. That is fine for composing!

"Now my work is finished and I have time to write, only I don't know what. I know of nothing new, excepting that number 35, 59, and 62 have been drawn in the lottery and if we had had these numbers we should have won, but since we have not entered, we have neither lost nor won, but have the laugh on the others."

It was in December, 1771, that Leopold and Wolfgang, now nearly sixteen, returned from Milan. The old Archbishop of Salzburg had died and a less popular one had taken his place. Wolfgang was now asked to write an opera for the installation of the new Elector, the Archbishop Hieronymous Colloredo. Already he had written over one hundred compositions, which included six symphonies, a Mass, piano sonatas, violin sonatas, trios, songs, religious works, quartets and operas.

Wolfgang's successes in Milan made Leopold hope Wolfgang might obtain a good position with the Grand Duke of Tuscany, or with the Empress's son, Ferdinand. But when Ferdinand asked his mother, the Empress advised against it, saying, "It is an unnecessary expense."

So at a tiny wage Wolfgang had to stay on in Salzburg in the employ of the Archbishop. The older he grew the more he disliked staying there. Leopold was greatly worried about Wolfgang's future, but there simply was no position elsewhere. The Archbishop began expressing his suspicions about Wolfgang's composing his own music, inferring it was Leopold who wrote it for him. To prove him wrong, Wolfgang undertook the composition of a cantata to words given him by the Archbishop. He was locked in some rooms of the palace with pens and ink and plenty of music paper until he had completed it. This satisfied the Archbishop that it was Wolfgang and not Leopold who was writing the compositions.

One day the Archbishop told his musicians, Wolfgang among them, that he was going to Vienna and would take them along to give a concert in honor of a special occasion there. Wolfgang was happy at the opportunity it would give him to see his friends in Vienna and, perhaps, give some concerts of his own. But in Vienna, when Wolfgang requested permission to give concerts, the Archbishop refused. Irritated, Wolfgang wrote to his father:

> "You see, Papa, I am not at all popular with the Archbishop, and I am wasting my time staying in Salzburg. He is tyrannical and annoyed that we are not subservient and obsequious like the other musicians. I would like to try elsewhere again."

Wolfgang was beginning to wonder why, despite all his successes in Europe, he had never been able to obtain a position outside of Salzburg. He wanted to go on a concert trip with his father again, but the Archbishop refused them leave of absence.

So Wolfgang applied for permission to make a concert tour

by himself, but the Archbishop was very unpleasant about it. He threatened Wolfgang with losing not only his own position, but that of his father as well. Still, Wolfgang insisted on going and handed in his resignation, to the annoyance of the Archbishop, who became insulting, calling Wolfgang's tours, "nothing but begging expeditions."

Even though he knew he was risking his own position at court, Leopold gave Wolfgang his consent to leave Salzburg. "I regret very much that I cannot go with you," he said, "but your mother will accompany you on this trip. It is plain enough that the Archbishop does not appreciate your accomplishments; though he has given you a few commissions, he had paid you practically nothing for them."

"But, Papa, why should Mama go with me? After all, I am twenty-one years old. It will look ridiculous for a person of my age to be traveling with his mother."

"It is not at all ridiculous, Wolfgang," said Leopold firmly. "Mama can look after your needs and thus leave you free for your music. You have never had to decide or manage things for yourself because I have always done them for you. If you do not agree to go with Mama, you will have to stay in Salzburg."

That was how it had to be, so Wolfgang no longer protested. In great detail Leopold arranged every stage of the trip, telling him which German towns and cities to visit and on what date he should reach Paris.

Like the obedient son he was, Wolfgang accepted his father's advice and suggestions, and set forth with his mother.

13

Paris

Wolfgang's first letter to his father and sister said:

"We both beg Papa to take care of his health, to laugh heartily, be merry and always joyful, remember, as we do, that the Archbishop is a rat, but that God is compassionate, charitable, and loving."

In Munich Wolfgang played for the Elector as well as at the homes of nobles. He did everything to interest them — giving concerts at court, competing with musicians from other countries to amuse the Elector. But it was all no use. Unfortunately, there never seemed to be any vacancy into which he could be appointed. He wrote to his father:

"I have an inexpressible desire to write an opera again — composition is my one and only passion and joy. I only have to hear an opera or go into a theater and hear them tuning up to be almost beside myself."

According to Leopold's itinerary, Wolfgang's next stop was Augsburg, where his father had been born and still had many relatives. Somehow, Wolfgang was not a success there. The local aristocracy did not take him seriously; they even made fun of him. Wolfgang's feelings were hurt, and he wrote home angrily about it. However, he very much enjoyed being in his uncle's house and having fun with his cousin Bäsle, a high-spirited girl. He wrote:

"O, I shall be honestly glad to go off again to a place where there is a court. I may say that if it were not for my good uncle and aunt and my really charming cousin, I should have as many regrets at having come to Augsburg as I have hairs on my head. I must now say a few words about my dear little cousin but I shall save that up until tomorrow. . . . Our little cousin is beautiful, intelligent, charming, clever and gay. . . . We two get on extremely well, for like myself, she is a bit of a scamp. We both laugh at everyone and have great fun."

It was in Augsburg that Wolfgang became acquainted with the famous organ-builder and pianoforte maker, Andreas Stein. He was so taken with the man and his instruments that he wrote Leopold telling him about the trouble and care Stein took with his instruments, and what a passionate lover of music he was. Wolfgang tested the various instruments, and when he tried out Stein's organs, Stein was amazed by young Mozart's understanding of how to play an organ like an organist, and not like a pianist.

The next place on Leopold's list was Mannheim, the seat of the Elector Palatine. (The Electors were the German princes who were entitled to vote in the election of the Emperor.) The court of the Elector Palatine was a center of art and music, chiefly to provide pleasure and amusement for himself; his orchestra was considered one of the finest in Europe. The Elector was also proud of his famous theater.

In Mannheim Wolfgang became acquainted for the first time with the clarinet as an orchestral instrument. He wrote to his father describing how beautiful it was, and how well it mingled with the oboe. He also wrote a concerto for it. He performed his six piano sonatas for the Elector's musicians.

After he left Mannheim Wolfgang wrote Bäsle a letter:

"Dear Coz Fuzz!

I have received reprieved your dear letter, telling selling me that my uncle carbuncle, my aunt can't and you too are very well. . . . Thank God we too are in excellent health wealth. Today the letter etter from my papa Ha! Ha! dropped safely into my claws paws. I hope that you too have got shot the note dote which I wrote to you from Mannheim. If so, so much the better, better the much so. Now for some sense."

Anna Maria wrote to Leopold:

"Wolfgang is made much of everywhere. Everyone says who hears him that his equal is not to be found. He plays whatever is put before him and [also] out of his head."

110

But like his other successes, this one did not bring in much money nor any offers from a patron. Wolfgang got so many watches as gifts that he wrote home:

"Let me tell you that I now have five watches. I have a good mind to have an added watch pocket made on each of my trousers so that when I visit some great lord it may not occur to him to present me with another one."

In a mixture of French and German, Wolfgang wrote many letters to his "little cousin" in Augsburg, making jokes and saying all kinds of naughty and nonsensical things to make her laugh. One day he wrote:

February 28, 1778

"My Very Dear Cousin,

"Perhaps you think that I am dead? Not at all. Don't believe it. Well, to make a long story short, about four hours from here — I have forgotten the name of the place — at some village or other, was a peasant, or shepherd, who was well advanced in years but was still hale and hearty. He was unmarried and very comfortably off and led a jolly life.

"But before I finish my story I must tell you that when he spoke he had a dreadful voice so that when he said anything people were always terrified of him. Well, to make a long story short, you must know that he had a dog called Bellot, a very fine large dog, white with black spots. Now one day the shepherd was walking along with his sheep, of which he had 11,000 and was carrying in his hand a stick with a beautiful rose-colored ribbon. For he always carried a stick. It was his habit to do this. Well, let's get on.

"After he had walked for a good hour or so, he got tired and sat down near a river and fell asleep and dreamt that he had lost

111

his sheep. He awoke in terror, but to his great joy found all his sheep beside him. So he got up and walked on, but not for very long; for he had hardly walked for half an hour before he came to a bridge which was very long but well-protected on both sides in order to prevent people from falling into the river. Well, he looked at his flock and, as he was obliged to cross the river, he began to drive his 11,000 sheep over the bridge.

"Now please be so kind as to wait until the 11,000 sheep have reached the other side and then I shall finish my story. I have already told you that no one knows how the affair is going to turn out. But I hope that before I send you the next letter the sheep will have crossed the river. If not, I really don't care very much; as far as I am concerned, they could have remained this side of the water.

I am your same old faithful cousin,

W. A. M."

No position was forthcoming in Mannheim, but Wolfgang did not worry because now he had become acquainted with a re-markable girl of fifteen, Aloysia Weber, a beautiful singer whose father was a music-copyist and musician. She sang the songs Wolf-gang composed so exquisitely that he fell in love with her and wrote his father that he would like to go on a concert tour with her, accompanied by her parents and three sisters. They could give such wonderful concerts together in Switzerland, Holland, and Italy, he wrote enthusiastically. He also informed Leopold he would much prefer not going to Paris.

When Leopold heard this he was very displeased. Wolfgang was not heeding his advice, not carrying out the careful plan he had worked out for him. He became suspicious of Aloysia's family, of their influence on his son. How could the girl be worthy of Wolfgang when she came from a family of such low cultural level? It was unthinkable!

There were many strong letters to Wolfgang and his mother from Leopold. His son was to give up the silly idea of touring with the Webers and go directly to Paris. Trying to reason with his beloved father, Wolfgang wrote:

> "We poor humble people can not only choose a wife whom we love and who loves us, but we may, can and do take such a one, because we are neither noble nor highly born, nor aristocratic, nor rich but on the contrary lowly born, humble and poor; so we do not need a wealthy wife, for our riches, being in our brains, die with us — and these no man can take from us unless he chops off our heads, in which case — we need nothing more."

But finally, Wolfgang thought it over and decided he had better do as his father wished. In March, 1778, when he was twenty-two years old, he set out with his mother for Paris, and, after a long, tedious journey of nine and a half days, arrived there.

Anna Maria had never liked Paris, and now that their living quarters were so much poorer than on their visit fourteen years before, she felt lonely and miserable. Melchior Grimm, the friend and compatriot who had been so kind in the past, tried again to be helpful and gave Wolfgang introductions to some of his aristocratic friends.

At the home of a duchess to whom Wolfgang had a letter of introduction he was kept waiting in a cold room a long time until she would see him. Then, when he played, she was inattentive because of some visiting gentlemen. Wolfgang had all he could do to keep from storming out angrily.

The opportunity to attend French opera, however, compensated somewhat for being away from his dear Aloysia. His father was informed that Wolfgang was offered a position as organist at the court in Versailles but he refused it. "Although I consider the organ to be the King of Instruments," wrote Wolfgang, "it is humiliating to be offered so little for my services."

He composed a ballet on commission, but kept wishing someone would ask him for an opera. It was something he could do so easily and happily!

Anna Maria complained of being very cold, of not feeling well. She was miserable and lonely in her small uncomfortable room, with Wolfgang often away all day giving lessons or performing at the homes of aristocrats. How she longed to be at home with her husband and Nannerl, in her own house where she would be warm and cozy, among the beautiful mountains, close to the lovely river winding through the town of Salzburg! Oh, if only she could hear the sound of her own language around her again!

Wolfgang grew anxious when he noticed his mother's failing spirits and declining health. He tried to cheer her and offered to call in a doctor. "I have no faith in French doctors and won't have one in the house," she told him firmly. By the time Wolfgang was able to find a German doctor, Anna Maria's condition had grown worse. Despite everything Wolfgang tried to do for her,

Anna Maria died at the age of fifty-seven. Wolfgang was overcome by the unexpected loss of his beloved mother. He did not know how to break the terrible news to his father. Finally, he decided the best thing to do was to write to a good friend in Salzburg, a priest, begging him to

". . . act the part of a true friend by preparing my poor father very gently for this sad news. May God give him strength and courage so that, when he hears the worst, he may not take it too hardly. I commend my sister to you also with all my heart. Use every means to comfort them. . . ."

Melchior Grimm was sorry for Wolfgang and invited him to come and live in his house. He lent him small sums of money until he could find enough pupils for music lessons. But he was not always pleased at Wolfgang's lack of aggressiveness, and he wrote Leopold saying:

"Wolfgang is too little concerned with the means by which one may become successful. Here, to make your way, you must be shrewd, enterprising, bold. One way of getting on here is to give music lessons, but it is fatiguing to run about Paris, and this occupation prevents him from composing, which he prefers to everything else."

Wolfgang kept hoping something good would turn up in the way of a court position. While he waited, he received a commission from a Dutch gentleman of means for three short simple flute concertos and a couple of flute quartets. Wolfgang wrote Leopold about it.

"It is not surprising that I have not been able to finish them, for I never have a single quiet hour here. I can compose only at night so that I can't get up early as well; besides, one is not always in the mood for working. I could, to be sure, scribble off things the whole day long, but a composition of this kind goes out into the world, and naturally I do not want to have cause to be ashamed of my name on the title page."

Another nobleman, who studied composition with Wolfgang and enjoyed playing the flute, had a daughter who played the harp. He asked Wolfgang to write a flute and harp concerto for them. Now Wolfgang also had a commission for a Sinfonie Concertante for flute, oboe, bassoon and orchestra. But even with these commissions, Wolfgang felt he was getting nowhere in Paris, and he wrote his father telling him this.

Leopold had begun to think that Wolfgang ought to come back to Salzburg, especially now that there happened to be a vacancy in the Archbishop's orchestra. Perhaps he could tempt him to return more willingly if he used Aloysia as a lure. He wrote Wolfgang that he should return for a court position and that he probably could get Aloysia a position as court singer.

This interested Wolfgang, and he decided to go to Mannheim and see Aloysia about it. However, before he went he discovered she had gone to Munich to be court singer at a high salary. He was glad for her good fortune, but it made it more difficult to go home without her.

Anyway he determined to stop off in Mannheim to see the Webers, whom he liked so much. When he got there, he found

116

that they too had gone to Munich with Aloysia! More than ever, the thought of returning to Salzburg galled him.

He kept delaying his journey back while angry letters from his father urged him to be on his way. Despite this, Wolfgang made up his mind to go to Munich to see Aloysia and the Webers. They would surely be glad to see him. But to his bitter surprise, he found that Aloysia, with her success, had completely changed toward him. While she admired him as a musician and composer, she was no longer interested in him as a suitor.

Wolfgang was very unhappy. Everything seemed to be against him, and now he did not know what to do. If it had not been for Aloysia's younger sister, Constanze, who had always been fond of him and now showed him her loving sympathy, he would have been overwhelmed with sadness. She did her best to console Wolfgang, and somehow, before he knew it, he was paying court to her and teaching her to play the harpsichord!

Vienna

14

Unfortunately there was no longer any excuse for putting off the journey home. To ward off his father's displeasure because of his delay in returning to Salzburg, Wolfgang stopped off in Augsburg and persuaded his lively cousin, Bäsle, to go home with him for a visit. He hoped her jolly presence would help matters, make life a little gayer there, make them all less conscious of the gap left by his mother's death.

When Leopold saw his cherished son again, he forgot about his anger and gave him a warm and loving welcome. Wolfgang now became the reluctant employee of the Archbishop, playing in the court orchestra and composing the necessary pieces needed for special occasions. Before long he learned that the Archbishop was planning to go to Vienna with some of his court musicians and Wolfgang was chosen to be among them. He was overjoyed at the opportunity to travel again and especially to revisit the city he liked so much.

Shortly after arriving in Vienna, Wolfgang asked the Archbishop for permission to play at the houses of friends, but he rudely refused Wolfgang's request. It annoyed Wolfgang that the Archbishop should have been so unreasonable and impolite, and he wrote his father about it expecting him to be sympathetic and understanding. But instead, he found Leopold siding with the Archbishop! It was the first time his father had failed him, and he sent him a letter.

> "I do not know what to write, my dearest father, for I cannot and never will be able to recover from my astonishment while you continue to think and write as you do. I must tell you I don't recognize a single trait of my father in your letter . . . a father, certainly, but not the best, most loving father, considerate of his own and his children's honor — in a word, not *my* father."

Wolfgang handed in his resignation to the Archbishop, determined to stay in Vienna, come what may. He was twenty-five years old and could manage his own life!

Now that he was living in Vienna, he hoped he would be able to get a permanent position either at court or with some noble family. Until then, he could give music lessons, perform at concerts, write music to order for whatever occasions arose. It would bore him to teach uninspiring, stumbling pupils, but until he obtained a good position he felt that with six pupils at what amounted to about a dollar a lesson he could support himself and not have to depend entirely on his father to send him money from time to time.

One of Wolfgang's pupils was a doctor. He left an account of his first lesson with Mozart. " 'Now play me something,' said Mozart. I played a fantasia of his own composing. 'Not bad,' he said. 'But now listen to me playing it.' It was a miracle. The piano became another instrument under his hands."

The Emperor, who had always thought highly of Wolfgang's ability as a composer and improviser, asked him to enter a contest with the pianist-composer, Clementi. It was a sport that amused the court. It was very easy for Wolfgang to win the contest, but while it brought him applause, it brought no profit. How much he preferred to compose music instead of being asked to enter such contests! If only he were given the opportunity to write down the music that constantly danced within his head, demanding to be released for all to hear and enjoy!

Often friends asked, when he complained about this, "Then why don't you put down on paper the music which lies ready in your head without waiting for a commission?"

Somehow, Wolfgang could not bring himself to do this, except to show his fitness for a position or to use as a composition for his own concerts.

His interest was turning more and more to the fortepiano, the forerunner of the modern piano, which he had first seen and tried in Stein's workshop in Augsburg, and now again in Vienna. Wolfgang was delighted with this new kind of keyboard instrument. The hammers, covered with leather, hit thin steel wires when the keys were pressed down. The keys, however, could not be pressed down as far as on the modern piano, and the wires were only half as thick. The swift contact and rebound from the string produced a clear, singing silvery tone. This kind of piano became known as the "Mozart piano" because Mozart used it so exclusively.

On December 15, 1781, Wolfgang had a surprise for his father. He wrote him that he wished to marry Constanze Weber! He described her virtues in the most glowing tones, saying that although she was not pretty, "she is the best-hearted, cleverest, and in a word, the best of the four sisters. She loves me and I love her truly." He went on to say that she understood housekeeping, that she was a good singer and played the harpsichord. He asked Leopold for his consent and blessing, and pointed out that marrying would lessen rather than increase his expenses because Constanze would take such good care of everything.

Leopold was far from pleased with the news. He certainly did not think Constanze good enough for his Wolferl, and he did his best to delay the wedding by withholding his consent. After waiting a month, Wolfgang decided to marry anyway, and he did so in August, 1782, hoping his father would relent. Not long after this Leopold's blessing came, but he made it plain that Wolfgang was to count on him no longer for any financial help. He pointed out that Wolfgang's decision to marry would now prevent him from ever being able to give material assistance to his sacrificing father in his old age.

Wolfgang's marriage took place about three weeks after he

had composed his opera *The Abduction from the Seraglio*. When it was performed at the old Burgtheatre, by royal command of Emperor Joseph II in honour of the Russian Grand Duke Paul's visit to Vienna, the Emperor told Wolfgang, with qualified approval, "My dear Mozart, too beautiful for our ears, and a terrible lot of notes!"

"Your Majesty, as many notes as are necessary," retorted Wolfgang with great self-assurance.

When he knew that Constanze was going to have a baby, Wolfgang felt more than ever the necessity of obtaining a permanent position. He thought of going to England, and even began taking English lessons to prepare himself. At the same time, to raise money for his family needs, he arranged subscription concerts for himself, writing piano concertos in which he would be the soloist, accompanied by an orchestra. Such concerts were usually his main source of income, and were well-attended by the Viennese nobility.

Very often when Mozart was busy composing and performing, he had to put off his pupils, thus reducing his income and plunging him still further into debt. How thankful he was to receive even the slightest of commissions to write serenades, divertimenti, or other light compositions for weddings, birthdays or anniversary celebrations, usually to be performed in parks or private gardens. He was grateful for any sum that would reduce his pressing bills.

Wolfgang was very eager for his father and Nannerl to see what a good and loving wife Constanze was. He was certain that

122

if they got to know her they would become better friends. So he wrote home that he and his wife were coming, and they set forth for Salzburg, where they stayed three months. While he was there, Wolfgang composed two duets for violin and viola as a favor for Michael Haydn, Joseph Haydn's brother. He was the Salzburg Cathedral's musician and composer, and when he was too ill to supply the necessary compositions, Wolfgang gave him his to pass off as his own in order to save him from losing his position.

Wolfgang was also writing a Mass in C minor, part of which was performed in the Salzburg Cathedral with Constanze singing the soprano solos. He told everyone he wrote the Mass in gratitude to God for his marriage to Stanzi.

Although the visit to Salzburg was fruitful as far as compositions were concerned, it did not bring the loving friendship he had hoped for between Constanze, his father, and Nannerl. Seeing that the strain among them could not be eased, Wolfgang and Constanze left Salzburg, saddened by their lack of success.

On their way back to Vienna they stopped off at Linz for a few days, during which Wolfgang composed the whole of one of his most beautiful symphonies, called the *Linz Symphony*.

Now they were back in Vienna again. Wolfgang was frequently invited to play in the homes of rich nobles who enjoyed giving private concerts with their own musicians, adding to them for a special occasion when needed. Wolfgang was very popular with them all, but somehow it never resulted in a desirable position for him. If only he had a wealthy patron who would give him a

regular sum, Wolfgang would gladly pour out all his compositions into his lap like a golden waterfall!

Many times Wolfgang was so in need of money that he had to ask his brother Masons for loans to tide him over. Mozart had joined the Masonic lodge in 1785. The mysticism of the ritual, the emphasis on friendship, the ideal of brotherhood in Freemasonry appealed to him.

Wolfgang had now composed his amusing opera, *The Marriage of Figaro,* which became a sensation in Prague, Bohemia. Despite its success it made no great material difference to Wolfgang, because operas were bought outright at what amounted to two hundred dollars, and no matter how long an opera ran, nothing more came to the composer but praise.

All too frequently, Nannerl wrote Wolfgang that their father was not well. This worried Wolfgang, and he wrote loving letters to Leopold about his health, emphasizing how much he wished he could help him financially. As it was, he had to confess, he could hardly take care of his own little family with the tiny sums he earned.

Within a month Nannerl sent Wolfgang the sad news that their father had died. With the loss of his father, Wolfgang's hopes seemed to diminish. It worried Constanze to see Wolfgang growing discouraged, for usually his high spirits sparkled and he was full of gaiety despite the frequent disappointments he suffered.

In the meantime, Joseph Haydn, called affectionately Papa Haydn by the musicians he conducted at the court of Prince

Esterhazy in Hungary, received an invitation from Prague asking him to write a comic opera for them. Haydn, who preferred to compose symphonies, quartets, and oratorios, responded:

"Why should you ask me for an opera so long as Mozart is alive? Such a great master can occupy the field alone. Ah, if only I could persuade every friend of music, especially the great ones, to understand and to feel Mozart's inimitable works as deeply as I do, and to study them with as great feeling and musical understanding as I give to them. If I could, how the cities would compete to possess such peerlessness within their walls!

"Prague would do well to keep a firm grip upon this wonderful man — but also to reward him with treasures. For unless they are rewarded, the life of great geniuses is sorrowful, and, alas, afford little encouragement to posterity to strive more nobly; for that reason so many promising spirits succumb.

"It angers me that this unique man, Mozart, has not yet been engaged by some imperial or royal court. Forgive me, honored sirs, for digressing, but I like the man too well . . ."

The friendship of Haydn and Mozart had first begun at the home of Haydn's friends, when Wolfgang was still a boy and some of his quartets were being played.

They had met again after many years, when Haydn was fifty-three and Wolfgang was twenty-nine years old. Both had the same tastes in music, with the greatest admiration for each other's compositions.

When Haydn and Mozart walked together in Vienna, whenever Haydn's Prince Esterhazy came to visit the city, they were

125

a curious-looking pair. Mozart, much smaller than Haydn, was lively and apparently carefree, sometimes dressed like a dashing cavalier, sometimes like a poor apprentice. His eyes sparkled when musical ideas came to him, and his whole manner was in deciding contrast to that of Haydn, who always behaved with great dignity and dressed very carefully.

Wolfgang sent Haydn his six quartets with a letter in Italian, calling him father, guide, and friend. "I learned from you how to write quartets. No one else can do everything, jest, shock, create laughter, and arouse profound emotion like you."

They were boon companions from 1785 to 1790, and if any-one dared to say a word against his idol, Wolfgang grew angry. He spoke of Haydn as if he were the great man's pupil, and when a musician criticised Papa Haydn's music, he said, "So you don't like Haydn's quartets? I tell you this, sir, if the two of us were joined into one, we would still be a long way from amounting to a Haydn."

At another time Kozeluch the composer said to Wolfgang, "I wouldn't have written the music the way Haydn did."

"Neither would I," said Wolfgang, "and do you know why? Because neither you nor I would have been so inspired!"

Although Haydn had already been a distinguished musician and composer when Mozart was a little boy, he behaved as if he were Wolfgang's disciple. It was often said that it was Wolfgang's genius that had inspired Haydn's famous London Symphonies. In Vienna people said admiringly, "On Monday Haydn writes like Mozart, and on Tuesday Mozart writes like Haydn."

126

At the time Leopold visited Wolfgang and Constanze in Vienna in 1785, Haydn said to him, "I, as an honest man, tell you before God that your son is the greatest composer I know, in person or by name."

15

Prague

In the spring of 1787, Mozart was told that a strange-looking lad, about sixteen years old, was downstairs with a letter of introduction to him from the Elector in Bonn. The young man was brought up to see him. Wolfgang saw a shy boy whose accent showed he was from the Rhine country. After reading the letter, Mozart said to him, "Welcome and good day, Herr Beethoven. I am delighted to see you and eager to hear you play."

Ludwig van Beethoven came forward shyly, bowed, and shook hands. Mozart led him into his music room and said graciously, "Please sit down here and play my piano. The letter you have brought recommends you highly. I should be happy to hear you play."

For a moment Ludwig sat meditatively; then he began to play.

For a short time Wolfgang listened with absorption, but suddenly he turned toward the window, looking outdoors. He had lost interest in the lad's playing, which had become excited, loud and fast, as if he were being chased by a fiend.

When Ludwig finished, he turned toward Wolfgang and to his dismay saw that his gaze was directed outdoors. Mozart must have been bored by his playing!

Ludwig waited for Mozart to speak, dejected by his painful silence. At last Wolfgang stood up and said, "Was what you just played something you prepared especially for me?"

"Yes, sir, but I see it did not please you. Please do not judge me yet. If you will but give me a few notes of music, I'll improvise for you. That is what I like to do best, and I have been told that I excel in this kind of music. Please give me another chance."

Not wishing to leave the lad completely discouraged, Mozart walked over to the piano and half-heartedly played a few notes.

Eagerly young Beethoven seized the few notes Wolfgang had set down and began teasing the phrase. At first he was gentle with it, tasting it; then, as if he realized the notes were in his power, the music grew in strength and joyousness.

Wolfgang's interest returned; he now sat forward, straining to hear and see. What a style of playing this young fellow has, what heart he shows in the soft, slow passages! There *is* something special about this lad from Bonn. More and more astonished at what he heard, Wolfgang came closer to the piano to study the musician's transformed face. Ludwig's whole stormy character was revealed as he improvised, weaving one lovely melody and phrase into another, and at last winding up with a burst of passion.

Finished, Ludwig took out his handkerchief to wipe his perspiring face. Before he had time to wonder what his idol would say, Mozart seized his hand, full of enthusiasm. Ludwig looked up, almost imploringly. As through a mist he heard Mozart shouting, "Bravo! Splendid! Well, Beethoven, if you wish to study with me, it will be an honor to teach you what I know. Come tomorrow morning at ten o'clock and bring all your compositions with you. It will be a pleasure to work with you."

Ludwig's face was radiant. Bowing respectfully, he said, "Thank you, sir. I shall be here promptly at ten o'clock. Oh, there is so much for me to learn!"

Wolfgang was greatly interested in young Beethoven, and charged him almost nothing for the music lessons, though he himself was in great need of money. The lad had begun composing the lovely Trio in E flat for piano, violin and cello and to Mozart that was more important than his fee.

He had given Ludwig only a few lessons, however, when one day a message was left for Wolfgang while he was out, saying that the lad from Bonn had called and said, "A letter has come from my father urging me to return home immediately because my mother is seriously ill. Perhaps I shall be able to come back to Vienna later, but if not, I thank the Master for his great kindness and generosity. Please tell him that I shall never forget what he has done for me, never!"

Wolfgang was very sorry to lose such a pupil, and he told his friends, "Keep an eye on this Ludwig van Beethoven. You will hear about him some day."

At the end of January, 1787, Wolfgang left for Prague with Constanze to compose a new opera commissioned for a performance to be given the following season. For this he received payment of the usual two hundred dollars, after which the opera was no longer considered his property. On his return to Vienna, during most of that particular year, Wolfgang worked also on his opera *Don Giovanni,* as well as on quintets, songs, four-hand sonatas, a sonata for piano and violin, and some more serenades.

In September he brought his unfinished opera *Don Giovanni* to Prague and finished it while he and Constanze lived in a friend's country house in "Bertramka's vineyard." While they were guests in these happy surroundings they enjoyed good food, cheerful company, games of darts and skittles, and amusing conversation. Wolfgang often worked on his opera on the stone table in the garden, with ripening grapes near at hand, and fine views all about him. The Mozarts were in no hurry to return to Vienna. They were delighted to be away from their domestic cares. Constanze's new baby was not yet due, and little Karl was being taken care of by Stanzi's mother in Vienna.

The overture to *Don Giovanni* was written down only the night before the opera's performance in Prague. To complete it in time, Mozart had to work all through the night. "Sit by

me, Stanzi," he said to his wife, "and keep me awake by telling me stories."

Mozart's ability to write music even in a room full of people talking, dancing, laughing, or joking was the wonder of all who knew him. He never had to go to the piano, and he wrote with such great speed and ease that he seldom had to erase or improve a passage once it was written down on paper. His whole composition was clear in his head before he set it down.

In Prague on October 14th, 1787, an Italian opera company performed first the opera *Figaro,* and two weeks later, *Don Giovanni,* with Wolfgang conducting. Because of *Don Giovanni's* success, the Emperor Joseph II appointed him successor to the famous court composer, Gluck, but at a fraction of Gluck's salary. Gluck's salary had been two thousand gulden a year, Mozart's was only eight hundred. Although he was bitterly disappointed, Mozart was too deep in debt to protest. One day he attached this note to the receipt he signed for his meager wage, "Too much for what I do, too little for what I could do."

The Emperor Joseph did not ask him for any large works; he had Wolfgang write music for court balls, such as minuets, German dances, counter-dances, and light compositions for festive occasions.

Curiously enough, though *Don Giovanni* had been a great success in Prague, it was not in Vienna. The Emperor told the librettist, da Ponte, who had written the play for the opera: "*Don Giovanni* is divine, perhaps even more beautiful than *Figaro,* but it is not food for the teeth of the Viennese."

When Wolfgang heard this, he said, "Very well, give them time to chew."

Wolfgang's financial situation was not greatly changed by the successes of his operas, and to eke out a living he had to continue giving music lessons. He would tell his wife, "It is such a dilemma, dear Stanzi. If I have too many pupils, I don't have time to compose, and if I don't have any, I am too worried about our income to think of compositions."

He gave piano recitals privately and publicly, and during the years 1783-1786 he composed fourteen of his great piano concertos and other compositions, some for his own performances, some for his pupils. Many of his works were written for a famous performer or cherished friend. One of them, Leitgeb, a horn player, on whom Wolfgang liked to play jokes and for whom he wrote some lovely horn concertos, had to read from music written in blue, red, green and black inks.

Wolfgang often wrote charming concert songs and arias for singers who were friends of his. He could adapt his songs to fit the special qualities of a singer's voice and thus insure their success.

16

Vienna

Wolfgang's last three sym-
phonies were all composed within six weeks, during the summer
of 1788. To earn something quickly he also wrote waltzes, country
dances and compositions for mechanical clocks and organs, which
were very popular in the eighteenth century. The sizes of the
mechanical clocks and organs varied from small ones of exquisite
craftsmanship to large bizarre ones. Usually the cylinder was of
wood or metal which revolved slowly by a clockwork mechanism.
In it were inserted pins or pegs spaced out in a certain order, cor-
responding to the notes of music which the machine was to play.

As the cylinder revolved, the pins either came in contact
with a row of metal strings or the teeth of a metal comb, or
opened valves attached to small organ pipes into which air was

forced by bellows which worked the mechanism. A cylinder could give only a small number of tunes, the number depending on the size of the clock into which the cylinder was inserted.

Cylinder organs in Viennese restaurants were the juke boxes of that time and were very popular. Wolfgang was not the only one who composed for them. Carl Philip Emanuel Bach, J. J. Quantz, and Michael and Joseph Haydn wrote tunes for them also. Among the famous collectors of these ingenious clocks and organs were Marie Antoinette, Frederick the Great, and Napoleon.

In April, 1789, Wolfgang went to Berlin with his friend and pupil, Prince Lichnowsky. This trip was made to remind King Frederick William II that Mozart was still available for a court position. Frederick William was a music lover and played the cello. The king's predecessor, Frederick the Great, had also been a musician, an enthusiastic amateur flutist, the pupil of the court composer, J. J. Quantz, who composed over three hundred flute sonatas for Frederick to play.

Wolfgang found the visit to the musical king very pleasant, and he was asked to play often at court and at private houses. But again, no position resulted from the expedition, although he did receive an order from Frederick William for six string quartets and six easy piano sonatas for the princess, his daughter.

Wolfgang wrote to Constanze, whom he missed very much:

"Dearest Little Wife!

If only I had a letter from you! If I were to tell you all the things I do with your dear portrait, I think that you would often laugh. For instance, when I take it out of its case, I say, 'Good day, Stanzerl! Good day, little rascal, little turned-up-nose,' and when I put it away again, I let it slip in very slowly . . . and then, just at the last, quickly, 'Good night, little mouse, sleep well.' Well, I suppose I have been writing something very foolish (to the world at all events); but to us who love each other so dearly, it is not foolish at all. Today is the sixth day since I left you and by Heaven! it seems a year. Adieu, my only love! The carriage is waiting. Farewell, and love me forever as I love you."

On his return home the lack of money became so pressing that Wolfgang was forced to ask his fellow Mason, Michael Puchberg, a rich business man and lover of music, for loans of money.

"... If you, my best friend and brother [Brother Mason] forsake me, then I with my poor sick wife and child am blamelessly and lucklessly lost. Through my wife's unlucky illness I am deprived of my earnings."

Constanze, although a devoted wife, was not a very economical housekeeper, and because of Wolfgang's irregular earnings, the two of them were often thoughtless about what they spent. Even when he was at the peak of his popularity as a concert pianist, they were often penniless. Furthermore, with Constanze's numerous babies, four dying at birth, and only two surviving, their small funds were used up by medical expenses and frequent trips to Baden for the medicinal baths.

Puchberg received thirteen letters from Wolfgang appealing for money, and he never failed to lend him small sums to tide the Mozart family over an emergency. If it had not been for him, two of Wolfgang's greatest operas, *Cosi Fan Tutte* and *The Magic Flute* might never have been written, because when Wolfgang was overburdened with anxiety about money, he could not compose with any peace of mind.

One day during the winter, when it was particularly cold and money as scarce as ever, a friend came to see Wolfgang. What should he see but Wolfgang and Constanze dancing energetically!

"Are you teaching your good wife to dance?" asked the friend, surprised.

"Oh, no, my little wife and I are dancing only to keep warm," said Wolfgang.

The friend hurried out and soon returned with a present of a bundle of firewood.

Cosi Fan Tutte had been commissioned by Emperor Joseph II, but it was dropped from further performance after appearing ten times, despite the fact that some of Mozart's most beautiful melodies are in this opera. Music poured out of him so copiously that, if necessary, he could write a composition to order the very day it was to be performed.

In March, 1790, Emperor Joseph II was succeeded to the throne by Leopold II, and now Wolfgang was sure something good would come his way. The coronation would be in Frankfurt. He thought it would be useful to attend the festive occasion; perhaps he would be invited to play or given a commission for a piece of music. In order to pay his expenses on the trip, he had to pawn some of their household articles.

Although in Frankfurt Mozart met old acquaintances and

138

gave two concerts in the town theater with great success receiving both honor and glory, the trip was a failure as far as money was concerned. He wrote to Constanze:

"I am as excited as a child at the thought of seeing you again. If people could see into my heart, I should almost feel ashamed. To me everything is cold, cold as ice. Perhaps if you were with me I might possibly take more pleasure in the kindness of those I meet here. But as it is, everything seems so empty."

Later, while she was in Baden, he wrote:

"Dearest, Most Beloved Little Wife,
    You cannot give me greater pleasure than by being gay and happy, for if only I am certain that you are all right, then my troubles are light and easy; for the fatal and strained position I am in becomes a mere trifle if only I know that you are well and happy. Ever your loving husband,

Mozart

"See that Karl behaves himself. Give him kisses from me."

He did not have the heart to tell her that the family income was dwindling, because concert performances were becoming fewer and he now had only three pupils, the others having gone away to the country for the summer.

His persistent bad luck and scarcity of money were beginning to have an unhappy effect on him despite his naturally gay and cheerful disposition. One day a stranger dressed entirely in gray came up to him as he was about to leave Vienna to attend Leopold II's coronation as King of Bohemia. Wolfgang had been asked to compose a festival opera for the occasion. The stranger handed

Wolfgang fifty ducats and asked that he compose a *Requiem,* a Mass for the dead. He did not say who he was or for whom it was to be. Wolfgang, glad to have the money, quickly agreed, but he kept wondering who the mysterious stranger could be.

During his journey to Prague Wolfgang set to work on the new festival opera, *The Clemency of Titus,* and he managed to finish it in time for the performance. But even in Prague, where they adored Mozart's music, the opera was not a success. It was really not up to his own standard, partly because he was feeling ill and discouraged and was exhausted from the hurried trip.

When he returned to Vienna a few months later, although he was now in really bad health, he managed to complete *The Magic Flute,* for performance in September, 1791. This opera, very different from *Figaro* and *Don Giovanni,* was a new kind of opera, with roots deep in German life and ideals. Though like all his other great music, *The Magic Flute* brought little financial reward, it was an almost immediate triumph. Now Mozart set to work on the *Requiem.*

He sent a letter written in Italian to his librettist, Lorenzo da Ponte, who had been urging him to come and join him in London. Wolfgang wrote:

"I should like to follow your advice, but how can I do so? My head is confused, I reason with difficulty and cannot rid my eyes of the image of this stranger. I see him continually begging me, soliciting me, and impatiently demanding my work. I go on because composition wearies me less than resting. Besides, I have nothing more to fear. I know from what I feel that the hour sounds; I am on the point of expiring; I have finished before having enjoyed my talent. Life was so beautiful, my career began under such favorable auspices, but no one can change his destiny. Nobody can count his days, one must resign oneself; it will all be as Providence pleases and so I finish my funeral song. I must not leave it incomplete.

Mozart"

Again it was necessary for Constanze to go to Baden for her health and leave Wolfgang alone with his worries and mounting expenses. Nevertheless he sent her what money he could, with merry letters to keep up her spirits. It was in Baden that their youngest child, a son, was born.

When Constanze returned and saw how ill Wolfgang looked, when she heard him insisting that he was writing the *Requiem* for himself, she said anxiously, "You have been working too hard, darling, and there has been no one to take care of you while I was away. But now I am here, and I shall look after you with all my heart. Soon you'll be your gay, cheerful self again."

But Wolfgang knew it was not so. He was tired, very very tired, and so weak he could barely compose. At last Constanze realized that this was no passing illness. She sent for the doctor.

It was too late for a doctor to help. All any of Wolfgang's friends could do was make things easier for him. One day in November he collapsed completely. Constanze put him to bed. She was terrified when she saw how swollen his hands and feet were.

By now Wolfgang was too ill to write music. But the thought

142

of the *Requiem* was foremost in his mind. He talked to his pupil Sussmayr, who sat by his bed, giving the young man directions for the unfinished parts of the work.

Even as he was dying, friends came to sit by Wolfgang and tell him about the latest performance of *The Magic Flute*. Weak as he was, Wolfgang tried to sing some of the music.

The *Requiem* was not finished, and now Mozart knew he would die before it was done. He could scarcely make himself heard as he gave some final directions to Sussmayr. He said, "Did I not say I was writing this *Requiem* for myself?"

He never knew that the *Requiem* had been commissioned by Count Walsegg, an amateur musician who ordered compositions anonymously and then pretended to have composed them himself. The *Requiem* had been commissioned in memory of the Count's wife. As Wolfgang could not finish it, Sussmayr did it as much as possible in the way Mozart had indicated to him, and gave the *Requiem* to the count.

Mozart died on December 5, 1791. He was thirty-five years old.

In his brief life he had composed hundreds and hundreds of priceless compositions of great beauty. But all he could leave Constanze and their two little boys was about ten dollars, some books, and their simple household articles.

Constanze was so overwhelmed with grief that she could not attend the funeral of her husband. After a short service in the cathedral, his coffin was carried unescorted through a storm of rain and snow to the cemetery in the churchyard of St. Mark's.

Because of the severe December weather, not a single relative or friend was present at the burial, and since there was no money for a separate grave, Mozart's wasted body was buried in a common pauper's grave. Before long no one even knew where he had been buried.

His body was gone, but his magnificent music — symphonies, operas, duos, trios, quartets, violin concertos, piano concertos, vocal and choral works praising God, happiness, and all of life — lives forever.